Annoying Dead People

By

Evelyn Adams

Copyright 2015

Prologue

I am a Medium, or Psychic as some prefer to call it. The following are simply a set of 'life experiences' I have decided to share with you. Each chapter appears in no set order so don't think in terms of a timeline.

Open your hearts to new worlds of consciousness; which is simply to say let wisdom and truth guide you through this journey you have placed yourself upon.

Evelyn Adams

Chapter One

Applying for a job online I was called in for an interview. I will not name this corporation, just know it is very large and is involved in the hospitality industry in Florida.

I am a Medium or what many today simply call a Psychic, who sometimes feels compelled to use my gift's when those from the unseen world wish to communicate with those among the living, as it were. Being clairvoyant and clairaudient; which simply means I can see and hear the dead as some folks refer to them; I prefer to call them spirits. Because of my abilities the dead can and quite often do show up at the most inopportune of times, which can be annoying to say the very least. So, I just try and go with the flow and see what happens.

The Human Resource person; a very nice, well spoken lady who seemed to be in her early to middle thirties came into the waiting area and called my name. We exchanged pleasantries as she led me back to her office.

Sitting down inside her small office which contained only two chairs and a small desk she first looked over my resume and then began the interview process.

"I'm Maria Hernandez, and I see here that you have applied for the front desk customer service position, is that correct?"

"Yes, I'm very comfortable when dealing with all types of people, no matter what their culture or nationality might be."

"Tell me what did you least like about your last job?" she continued.

As she finished that question, I could now psychically see an older woman who was now standing to her left side. My first thoughts were; please go away, I really need this interview to go well, I need the income, and I mentally relayed that information to the elderly woman.

The older lady smiled and said she truly needed to make contact with my interviewer. She stood there, her form radiating peace and compassion, yet her eyes showed the desperation in her need to make contact. Knowing full well from past experience what might happen if I make her presence known, I still felt compelled to try.

"Did you not understand my question?" Maria asked politely. She had taken notice that I was staring at what appeared to her as the blank wall on her left side. She at one point momentarily glanced to her left to see what I might be looking at.

I broke off looking at the older woman and then answered her. "I'm so sorry, but this may seem very strange, but there is an elderly woman standing by your left side…she is telling me her name is Camila and that she is your mother. She is wearing a blue dress with a red rose pinned on it. She also has a white hat with a short white veil."

Maria looked to her left again, then back to me. "I beg your pardon. How do you know my mothers' name?"

"Camila is saying how sorry she is for not coming to your wedding…that she truly thought Alfredo was not the man for you to marry. She felt in her heart he was no good and would cause you great harm. But now from the other side she can see into his heart and she sees the love he has for you. She now knows he would never harm you or the children. She is asking for your forgiveness…"

Maria had a very surprised look upon her face, to say the very least. "Is this a joke?" Maria asked in a serious tone. "How dare you bring up the memory of my mother…you have no right…this interview is over. You need to leave, and I mean right now!"

Maria had tears welling up in her eyes; I could tell there was a lot of emotional baggage she was still carrying around from her relationship with her mother. "Your mother wants you to know…"

"Get out right now…I will call security if you don't leave right now!" she threatened as she picked up the phone.

As I went out the door I looked back and Maria was now sitting, her face buried in her hands as tears rolled down her cheeks between the soft sobs.

Getting into my car I couldn't help but think; there goes another good job...I hope Camila is happy now, because no one else is.

Early the next morning there came a knock at my front door. I opened it to find a man in his late thirties who had a very serious expression on his face.

"Are you the one who came to see my Maria yesterday?" he said speaking very rapidly. "Don't lie; I know you're the one who upset my Maria!" he burst out yelling.

"I'm sorry, who are you?" I asked softly through my shaky voice.

"I'm Alfredo, her husband." His voice was gruff and angered.

"I was only trying to…" he cut me off in mid-sentence.

"You're a goddamn witch! That's what you are…stay away from my Maria!" He screamed as I closed and locked my door.

His rage was strong, before returning to his car he yelled through the door, "You will burn in hell!"

My hands were trembling, and I had trouble catching my breath. I wasn't sure what Maria had said to her husband about our conversation the day before, but I have had similar reactions like this before. But this is the first time anyone came to my home. I guess Maria let her husband see my resume which contained my address and other personal information.

Three days later I received a phone call; to my surprise it was Maria Hernandez. She wanted to apologize for her husbands visit to my home. Apparently after she informed him of what took place several arguments ensued between them and some other family members as well.

I told her it was not my intention to cause her, or her family any stress or grief concerning her deceased mother. I wasn't really that surprised when she asked if I was a psychic and could she come to my home for a private reading to discuss

Camila. I said it would be fine and we set a date and time.

Two days later in the evening I heard her pull into my driveway. I invited Maria in, and I put out a bowl of potato chips and we each had a glass of cold Pepsi poured over ice.

"I wish to apologize for my husbands' behavior; his beliefs come straight from the Catholic faith as do many of my other family member's beliefs.

My two younger sisters however do not follow the old religion; they call themselves 'spiritual, but not religious' as many of the young do in today's world. I too do not follow the old religion.

After much discussion they have convinced me to listen to what you have to say; to not let my fear keep me from the truth."

I thought to myself that when Maria said 'after much discussion' she really meant to say after much yelling and arguing between the family members she decided to call me.

"Your husband did frighten me I must admit, but you don't owe me an apology. I knew when I started to tell you about your mother things might get ruff. So, let's just start with a clean slate." I said smiling.

"Do you want money from me?" Maria asked in a low voice.

"Oh, heavens no, I only told you about your mother because she wouldn't stop pestering me during the interview." I was surprised as we both laughed.

"Yes, that was my mother alright; she never knew when to stop talking." We again laughed together.

"I hope you are prepared…" I said looking over her right shoulder.

Maria looked at me then turned to look behind her. "Is she here now?"

"Yes, she is."

Maria started to cry softly as she turned to face me, "Please tell her I forgive her."

"She can hear you, so you may say whatever you wish." I said in a reassuring tone. "Camila is saying how sorry and how wrong she was about Alfredo and that she only wanted what was best for you. She loves you very much."

Maria was wiping tears from her eyes, "I love you too very much Mama."

I now could see standing next to Camila a little boy, he looked to be about four years old it seemed to me. He was holding Camila's hand and was smiling. Mentally I asked Camila who the little boy was. She said it was Maria's little boy. I asked what his…

"What is my mother saying?" Maria interrupted my thought.

"Well, there is a small boy who is about four year's old standing by your mother. She says he is your son."

"What…my son…how can that be? I have two daughters, and both are alive! I have no son. I don't understand?" Maria seemed completely caught off guard by her mothers' statement.

"Your mother says you became pregnant four years ago and you did not want another child; that your two sisters took you to a clinic where you underwent an abortion. You did not want Alfredo to know so you all swore yourselves to secrecy. You felt your husband would not understand due to his strong belief in the church ways. Your mother says you do not believe in the Catholic faith because she raised you in another faith. She says you only became Catholic to please your husband and his family."

Hearing this sent Maria off the couch as she fell onto her knees sobbing uncontrollably. I rushed to her side trying to console her. After several minutes she regained her composure and got up from the floor and sat back down.

Maria explained she felt she did not have the time or strength to take care of another child. She was afraid to tell her husband, so she told her sisters who said they would support her decision and help her make arrangements to go to the clinic in another city. Alfredo had left to go work at a construction site in another state during this time.

She did not know the tiny fetus was even a male she said in between bouts of crying. Maria asked if her mother and the boy were still present in the room, and I told her yes, they were still here.

"Please ask my mother what she calls my son?" Maria asked in a calm voice.

"The boy, she said, named himself; he is called 'Alfredo Benito Hernandez, Jr.', he took his fathers name. They simply call him 'Junior' and your mother says he loves you very much. She said he comes at times and sits next to you and holds onto your arm to express his love for you. She says you have felt this before, have you not?"

"Oh my God…yes, yes I have, I never knew what it was, but I would feel so calm when I felt that odd sensation as if something was completely embracing my arm." She was smiling and looking off into the distance as it were; seeing and experiencing the love and gentle comfort the little boy had brought to her.

"Junior says on his birthday he would be so joyous if you would buy him a birthday balloon and release it in the small park down the street from your house." I said as Maria's gaze fell back upon me.

"Oh yes, tell Junior I will from now on...each and every birthday, I swear it!" An odd look came over her face as she asked this question, "Please ask Junior…when is his birthday?"

He answered before I could send the thought; I wasn't sure how Maria was going to react to his answer, "His birthday is the day you aborted him on, he says you know that day very well." Maria looked stunned, and then burst into tears again. I gave her more tissues and waited while she processed that statement from her son.

Camila now spoke to me and I relayed everything she said to Maria verbatim, "Abortion is not a sin as many religions upon the earth may claim. It is simply a lesson for many to learn to understand this great choice. Abortion will never completely be understood in this physical world you inhabit. There are no unfavorable circumstances when deciding to have an abortion or to not have an abortion. There should be acceptance of this practice; though the goal should be to overcome the fear associated with it by those who are wishing to carry it out. Overcome the worry, fear and selfishness you place upon yourselves because of this act. Your son chose you as his mother knowing full well that you would abort him, this was his choice too. He came to experience this short life in your womb for his personal spiritual growth. You may never fully understand his decision during this lifetime, but you will come to an understanding once you cross over and reunite with us. All will be made clear then. If you understand nothing else, just know, abortion is not a sin and God does not judge those who choose to bring this experience into their life path."

Maria stopped crying and said she needed to do some deep soul searching over what her mother had just expressed to her. She said she felt much better overall, but that she couldn't bring herself to tell her husband about Junior or the abortion. She was afraid of what he might do, so for now she would remain silent.

"Maria, your mother says she has one more thing to tell you and then they must go." I spoke very softly and reassuringly.

She gasped a little as I said that, "Oh my God, there's more?!" Her eyes were large and wide open with a look of mock disbelief. "I'm not sure I'm ready for this, I'm all cried out." She forced a little grin followed by a short chuckle as she slumped back into the chair.

"Don't worry dear, Camila said this is about your husband." I said smiling at her.

"Please don't tell me he's cheating on me?" A serious look befell her thin face.

"Oh no, this is nothing like that." I shot back which changed her negative facial demeanor immediately. "Your mother simply wants you to know that Alfredo is a very good-hearted man, even though he is quick to anger, he shall always be there for you and the children. Things you will discuss later in life; just remember to give him time to think about things. He is slow to make changes so just be patient with him."

"Yes, I understand." Maria said.

"There is one last thing she wants to say before she goes. Your mother says after she passed, her home was sold, and the money was divided among her living children."

"Yes, between me and my sisters, we all split it equally. It was not very much; we each got three thousand dollars." Maria said.

"Your mother says that you took her personal items, furniture and the like and placed it all in a large storage unit. She said you girls talked about one day getting together to go through her stuff

to decide what to do with it, but no one wants to

go there because of the sad memories of her

passing."

"Yes, that is true, we are having trouble letting

go I guess." Maria spoke from the heart.

"Your mother said she wants you and your

sisters to go to the storage unit. There in the far

back you will find an old chest full of family

photos from when she was a young girl. It is very

important that you go through this small chest;

she keeps repeating this to me, it is very important

she keeps saying. She wants you to promise her

you will do this for her." My voice was strong as

Camila's thoughts came with such force into my mind.

Maria looked at me first with surprise and then with conviction as she answered her mother's request, "Yes, I swear we will go and check out the family photos, just as soon as I talk with my sisters and we can work it out so that we can all go together."

"Your mother and son are now going to leave; they both expressed their great love for you and the rest of the family." I said as they vanished as quickly as they had appeared.

"I love you both so much!" Maria said, almost shouting as she placed her hands over her heart.

We chatted for a short time before she said she had to get home before her husband did, as she didn't want to explain where she had been. I completely understood as we parted company.

Three weeks had passed, and I was no closer to finding employment. I was making some money doing private readings here and there but that only paid for food and gas money. I was farther behind on my rent then I had realized; opening the mail I found an eviction notice from the management company. I had thirty days to leave or I'd be put out by the Sheriff's Department it read.

Talk about stress! It would be an understatement to say I was very worried and fearful. No relatives to fall back on as I was raised in an orphanage until I was eighteen and on my own from then on. I called my spirit guides and literally begged for their assistance, and then prayed to God to help me through this unnerving time in my life.

No longer a young girl, I didn't want to end up homeless; living and begging on the streets. I had some pretty ruff times when I was younger; sleeping in my car, washing up in gas station restrooms until I could get a waitress job or one cleaning homes. Working as a childcare worker at a group home, working with the mentally and physically handicapped and other low paid jobs was mainly all I could get with a high school diploma.

Finally, in my late twenties I saved up enough to go to one of those 'Certified Nursing Aids' classes. Pay was better than most of the other jobs I had. After thirteen years working many different nursing homes and hospitals as a 'CNA' I just couldn't handle the physical work anymore; my body was simply wearing out and exhausted.

I'm just a hair over five feet tall and only weigh one hundred and fifteen pounds on average; my thin build has been a disadvantage most of my life working as a CNA.

My last job was working as a waitress at a small corner restaurant. It paid the bills as long as

I kept to my budget. But when the last stock and housing markets and all that other stuff went south, I was laid off and the restaurant closed. I lived off the unemployment benefits until they ran out; now its sink or swim time I'm afraid.

There came a knock at my door in the late afternoon; as I opened the door not sure what to expect, Maria and two other women were standing there with great big grins on their beautiful faces.

She introduced her sisters to me and said she had told them everything that had happened and what their mother said when she came to see me. They had finally all gotten up the courage to go to the storage unit and face their fears and emotions.

I never expected so much excitement from them as Maria told me the details of their visit. They could hardly sit still as the story unfolded in my living room. Opening the unit brought back much grief and sorrow Maria said as they entered.

After a few minutes of tears and hugs she said they decided to find the little chest with the photos and take it to Maria's home so they could go through it there. They felt there was just too much sadness among all of their mothers' things to check out the photos in the storage unit.

Maria said to their great surprise not only were there family pictures inside the box, there were also U.S. Savings Bonds. Their mother and father had been buying one fifty-dollar savings bond every week for over thirty-five years; the total came to over one thousand eight hundred bonds.

They did some quick calculations online and said the bonds were worth over $200,000.00 dollars. You can imagine how ecstatically happy they were. It was as if they hit the lottery; hugs and kisses and joyous crying all around! I felt so overwhelmingly happy for them as they spoke of paying off their car and home loans and having money for their children's education and the like.

Maria also said they told their husbands who were dumbfound at first; then fully embraced their good fortune after the shock wore off. She went on to explain that her husband, Alfredo, asked why she all of a sudden decided to start going through the storage unit and she hesitantly confessed that she had come to my home and told him what had transpired concerning her dead mother. She did not mention Junior or the abortion.

She said he sat quietly and seemed to be pondering over what she told him all the while she braced herself for his short temper to show itself; but it was not forthcoming to her surprise. Another surprise came her way when several hours later he asked her to find out if he would be welcome to visit me and ask about his younger brother who died at age eleven due to a drowning incident.

I was truly surprised by this, but immediately told her he was more than welcome, and I would be glad to see if we could make contact with his brother.

The very next morning Maria called, and I agreed to see them that very same afternoon. Answering their soft knocking and before entering Alfredo came forth with such a heartfelt apology I was moved to tears. I could genuinely feel this man has such love and passion for his family that I accepted his apology without hesitation.

After entering Alfredo said he couldn't help but notice the eviction notice on the front door of my rented house. After making themselves comfortable we talked a little about my circumstances and then I noticed a young boy had appeared standing close to Alfredo and he told me he was his little brother, Julio, who had drowned.

Maria had noticed my attention was now focused as I gazed upon Julio. "Is he here?" she asked almost in a whisper.

Alfredo turned to Maria, "Is who here?"

She pointed at me and as Alfredo looked to my face I began to speak. "Julio is here and he wants you to forgive yourself Alfredo. He says the day he fell out of the fishing boat and drowned was a planned event in his short life. He knows you are going to have trouble understanding this, but he wants you to forgive yourself for not being able to save him."

Alfredo had tears welling up in his eyes as he spoke, "No, had I only moved faster I could have saved my little brother."

"Julio wants you to know that before he was born, he chose to live only a short time in this life and that he also chose the manner of his death. This was done for his spiritual growth, the growth of the true spirit being that he is. He did not need or require a longer life to experience the lessons he had chosen."

Alfredo suddenly had a strange look overtake his face, "You are saying Julio died on purpose...that he committed suicide? No, no, he was a good Catholic and suicide is a sin! This is a lie; it cannot be so! My little brother would never do such a thing!" Maria had wrapped her arms around her husband and was softly trying to calm him.

"Alfredo, Julio wants you to know he did not commit suicide, it was simply a planned event. He wants you to know that God gave his blessing to Julio for this short life he asked to experience." I said in a soft, reassuring voice.

"No! No, no, no…this is all a lie!" Alfredo took his wife by the wrist as he stood up and headed out the door. In the blink-of-an-eye they were gone.

My eviction date was only six days away so I was boxing up what I could fit into my car when there was a loud knock at my door. A wave of fear and panic flashed through me as I thought maybe I had misread the eviction notice and today was the day I was to be put out. I slowly peeked out the front window and to my surprise Maria was standing there with her two sisters.

After inviting them in Maria told me Alfredo had announced in the car on their way home the other day that they were to never speak of Julio or what had transpired in my home ever again. She said he is a good man, but he is a devout Catholic and he cannot go against the beliefs he was taught as a child and those beliefs of his family and friends.

I told her it was fine for him to believe whatever he wished; that we all have free-will and that we are all on a spiritual journey of self-discovery, which leads us to follow many paths in many lifetimes as we seek to know ourselves and to know God.

Maria and her sisters were all wearing big grins as one sister nudged Maria and said, "Go ahead, give it to her." Maria pulled an envelope from her purse and held it out toward me.

"Oh, no, you don't owe me anything. I told you from the start I wouldn't charge you for the readings. It was my wish to simply help, but now it looks like I may have caused you more problems and I am truly sorry if I made things worse."

Maria was no longer grinning, "You don't apologize to me or anyone else, you have helped me and my family in ways you will never know. We are so grateful to you for everything. Please take this gift, it comes from out hearts. We will not take no for an answer," she said as she placed the envelope in my hand.

"Well, thank you so much, I do wish you all well…"

Maria and her sisters were grinning again. You could almost feel their excitement as Maria spoke, "So, open it already!" They were like a bunch of giddy schoolgirls who just saw a celebrity at the Mall.

As I opened the envelope and pulled out the check, I was overcome by what I saw and burst into joyous tears. The check was for $5,000.00 dollars. We all hugged, and I cried for several minutes before regaining my composure. These selfless women went on to help me find a new place to live and also helped me with new employment as a cashier at a large supermarket.

Words truly could not express how happy and truly loved these beautiful women had made me feel!

* Note to Readers: I do psychic readings to help off-set my meager income. My spirit guides have always helped me with any financial problems that have popped up from time to time. You never know how they do it but when dire money problems have come to me, they always seem to work things out to where I end up okay.

Our spirit friends and guides are not here to make us rich or wealthy, but they do provide opportunities in order to assist us with completing our chosen lessons and life experiences.

Chapter Two

Earlier in the week I had received a phone call from one of my steady clients as I prefer to call them. A steady client is simply one that comes for a reading every few months or so. She said she had a friend who wished to make an appointment to get a reading from me. I agreed and made arrangements to see her friend that afternoon.

It was a rainy day; mostly scattered showers here and there which helped lessen the humidity and heat. She arrived a little early which was fine with me. We settled in; I usually just have my client sit next to me on my soft little couch. That seems to work best for me, I can pick up on their vibration as I tune into my guides.

When I'm not giving readings, I meditate three days a week for one hour and tune into my spirit guides as I seek to raise my vibration level and form an even better connection to the unseen world.

I do not use tarot cards now or other things of that nature to give a reading. When I first started out tarot cards were a great help to me, they gave me focus and reassurance that what I was receiving from my guides was accurate. But as time passed the strong bond which has developed with my spirit guides, I found I no longer needed the cards assistance in giving a reading.

She told me her name was Donna and she looked to be in her late fifties or possibly in her early sixties if I had to guess. Short, no more then five foot or so and very heavy for her height. She had some difficulty breathing at times but seemed very pleasant, yet she was perspiring a lot, so I asked if she wanted me to adjust the air conditioning to make it cooler, but she declined.

Donna said this was the first time she had ever gotten up the courage to go to a psychic. She said her family in general viewed psychics as fakes and people who prey upon the elderly and superstitious people in order to cheat them out of their money. I took no offense at her statement.

Then she brought up the question of what I charged for a reading and I explained for legal and tax reasons I do not charge, but simply ask for a 'love donation.' She asked how much the average person donates and I told her $30 dollars for thirty minutes was the average. I explained some give more; some give less depending on their financial circumstances and on the quality of the information they receive from my guides. She handed me $30 dollars and said she was ready to begin.

"So, Donna, I work in one of two ways. I can have my main guide I work with give you information that your spirit companions, those who watch over you in this life, wish you to have at this time and then you can ask questions or if you wish you can simply start asking the questions you are seeking guidance on. Your choice," I said pleasantly hoping to calm any fears she might harbor about talking to those on the other side.

"Oh, I have no questions for myself; I'm seeking some answers about the young man who saved Stephanie, my granddaughter three weeks ago." She said.

"Well then, let's see what my guides have to say about your granddaughter then."

"Yes, anything would be very helpful." Donna added.

After a few moments the information started pouring into my mind. "Was your granddaughter playing between your house and your neighbor's house with another little girl?"

"Yes, she was. She was playing with Ashley, my friend Geneva's little granddaughter. They are both five years old. We live on a dead-end street so the only people who come on the street are the ones who live there. No one else usually comes down our lane." She explained hurriedly.

"They are showing me a man of average height and weight who looks to be in his late forties. He is wearing jeans and a dirty T-shirt and has a slight beard and light-colored hair. He approached the girls and said he found a lost kitten and wanted the girls to come to his car to see if they knew who owned it." I said as the information kept coming from my guide.

"Yes, my next-door neighbor Geneva was coming outside to check on the girls when she saw the strange man talking to them and her description of him was the same as you just said. She yelled for the girls to come to her and Ashley ran to her grandma, but Stephanie was afraid and froze. Geneva yelled at the stranger that she was calling the police. The man then grabbed Stephanie and started carrying her to his car parked out front. Stephanie was now screaming and struggling my neighbor said but the man was too big and strong for her to break free of his hold. Geneva then said a younger man came out of nowhere and started fighting with the bad man, so she ran inside to call the police." Donna was now crying softly as she said this.

"They are showing me the stranger was trying to force her into the trunk of his car when a tall, dark haired man who looked to be in his early twenties ran up and grabbed the older man. The stranger let go of Stephanie while the two men fought with each other. The young man yelled for your granddaughter to run home which she did."

"Yes, she ran into the house and grabbed me around the waist crying, I asked her what was wrong, and she told me about the bad man and I immediately called 911 who said they already had units responding. I ran to the front door and locked it and peaked out the window. I saw the bad man driving off in a dark colored four door older model Buick. The police arrived a short time later and asked me and my neighbor for descriptions of the car and the bad man. The police said he was most likely a pedophile and that the young man my neighbor described saved my granddaughter from a terrible fate. But no one knew or had ever seen that young man on our lane before. He was nowhere to be found. He saved my Stephanie and I wanted to thank him for what he did." She said through her soft sobbing.

I handed her a box of tissue, "Are Stephanie's parents doing okay after this upsetting ordeal?" I asked very sympathetically thinking how scary

it must be to think someone almost took your

child from you.

Donna regained control of her emotions, "My

daughter Danielle had Stephanie when she was

twenty and the father, who was an asshole, left

before she was even born so he was never in the

picture. So, I was baby sitting one afternoon

when the police came and said a drunk driver had

ran a red light at a high rate of speed and slammed

into Danielle's car killing her. Of course, the

drunk lived, so I've been taking care of her ever

sense. My husband passed two years ago of a

sudden heart attack, so it's just me and Stephanie

now. So, I would truly like to know who the

young man was so I can give him my heartfelt thanks for saving my little Stephanie." She let out a deep sigh as tears welled up in her tired sad eyes again. One could tell she had experienced much sorrow in her life, yet she seemed to be holding up very well indeed. I sensed she had a lot of inner strength.

"Alright then, let me see if my guides can give me anything on the young man." After a few moments a flood of information came through to me. It was even a surprise to me what came through as I started to explain what had occurred.

First my guide explained for Donna that everyone, each spirit before they are born work up a blueprint, for a lack of a better word of what will take place in the life they are about to enter into. This blueprint contains lessons that the soul wishes to experience for its personal growth and enlightenment.

The nature of these lessons can come in many different forms. A spirit being may wish to experience, for example, the lesson of a disease such as cancer, diabetes or heart disease. They may choose to experience rape, murder or some type of sexual and/or verbal abuse and so on. These things are not to be viewed as negative things; just view them as experiences that cannot be experienced in the spirit world or that which many call heaven. Only here in the physical world do you have the opportunity to experience these events first had. I asked Donna if she understood so far and she said yes, so I continued on with the information my guide was sending me.

To simplify it for her, I explained that each person who is alive on earth have a spirit companion, some have several who watch over them and assist them with their chosen lessons. These spirit companions are called by many names. Some people say they have an Angel or Guardian Angel who watches over them, others seeking help call for Jesus, or for certain Saints, or for certain Archangels and the like.

The main focus of your spirit companion is to assist you in having the opportunity to experience the lessons you specifically chose for your personal spiritual development. Now understand that all spirits living in a human body have free-will. So even if you change the path you came to earth to experience, your spirit companion will still work behind the scenes, as it were, so that the lessons you chose still come to you.

Now, free-will also allows others to come into your life that you were not programmed to encounter. I explained to Donna that this was one of those moments in time. It was not a part of Stephanie's blueprint to experience being sexually molested and possibly murdered by a pedophile in this lifetime. My guide went on to say that when Stephanie's spirit companion was alerted by her vibrational change, due to her screams of distress immediate action was then taken by her spirit companion to stop this event.

The majority of the time your personal spirit companion will not interfere with your life because you have free-will. Only if it concerns death or certain other events will they intervene if the event is going to stop you from having the ability to learn your chosen lessons. The exception is, should you call out or mentally ask or pray for some kind of help or assistance then your spirit companion comes forth to assist you. For example, I explained to her that if you ask for guidance or for healing for yourself or for others your spirit companion then seeks to aid you with your request, because you asked for assistance.

Donna had a look on her face that told me she didn't understand all of this fully. "Is this making sense so far?"

"I'm not really sure what that all means. I just want to know about the young man." She said softly.

"Alright, let me see if they can tell me about him." I said as I sent the thought to my guide.

It wasn't long and the information came through. I began to tell her what my guide relayed to me. That the young man who came to the rescue as some might call it was not of this earth. Stephanie's spirit companion once alerted to the situation called upon higher beings to intervene in order to stop what was not programmed to occur in her chosen blueprint. A spirit being then was empowered by higher beings to penetrate into this world in order to stop the abduction of Stephanie by the so-called bad man. Once the spirit being stopped the event he simply returned to the unseen world. Sometimes these beings are referred to as 'walk-ins.' That is why no one had seen him before the event, and no one could find him after the event I explained.

"Oh, my goodness, so…in a way, it was God who sent one of his Angels to stop the bad man, is that right?" Donna asked trying to make sense of what I had just explained to her.

"Ah, yes, I guess you could say it that way."

I agreed.

"Thank you so much for your time, I better get home now. I can't wait to tell my neighbor Geneva about God sending an Angel to save my granddaughter," she said hurrying for the door.

* Note to Readers: A 'Walk-In' in the above-mentioned instance is a being that can be here temporarily, and they do not experience birth or death. There have been many instances when a walk-in intervened in an incident and later was never found or seen again. It is not some great mystery; life by physical means is simply a matter of bringing together the correct particles, atoms

and ions. It is not a matter of the stork bringing

into existence the necessary arrival. Now there

are walk-in's (Soul's) that do trade places with

Soul's who were born and are living a human life.

For whatever reason, a soul may decide it can no

longer continue its chosen lessons and with its

permission and the permission of a higher group

of spirit beings it can be removed from a physical

body and replaced with another soul who is

willing to finish up that lifetime.

Chapter Three

One evening I was relaxing and watching television when the phone rang. As I answered a soft female voice spoke.

"Hello, is this Evelyn the psychic?"

"Yes, it is how may I help you?"

"My name is Jody and my mother said I should call you about my youngest daughter Lisa." She went on to explain about her mother being one of my clients and that her mother felt the spirits could help with her daughters' problem.

"When would you like to come over for a ready?" I asked looking at my wall calendar. I make notations on my calendar, so I don't schedule too many clients on the same day. If I do more then six readings in a day, I get very

tired, so I try not to overdo it.

There was a short pause before Jody spoke, "Is

there any way you could read for me over the

phone? My mom said you charge thirty dollars

and I swear I'll send you the money but I'm so

worried about my little girl, she's only five years

old."

"Ah, sure, I can do that, can you hold on while

I get myself situated?"

"Please, take your time," she said waiting

patiently on the other end of the phone.

Sitting the phone down I then turned off the

television. Closing my eyes, I took in a deep

breath and held it for the count of seven then

exhaled and held that for a count of seven. I do this a total of seven times to relax my mind and body. Then I mentally call for my spirit guides. Picking up the phone, "Alright Jody, I'm ready. What is the problem or question you wish to ask about?"

"Lisa has these awful 'night terrors' where she wakes up screaming and crying and it's very hard to calm her down. I just don't know what to do. This happens a couple times a week now. I've taken her to two different pediatric doctors, and they say there's nothing medically wrong with her and one suggested taking her to a child psychiatrist. So, my question is should I take her to see a psychiatrist?" I could here the fear in her voice.

"Well, let me see what my guide has to say on this matter." Before I could mentally ask for the information, it was already flowing into my mind from my guide.

The main guide that works with and through me I call Alexander simply because I cannot pronounce his true name, he goes by in the spirit world. Names in the spirit world are different from those in the physical world we live in. He told me true spirit names are a combination of sounds and colors and can even convey emotions or smells which those in the human form cannot begin to understand.

So, as I said I simply asked him for a name I could pronounce and he said Alexander was a name he was called by during a lifetime he lived in the physical form many, many centuries ago before our current history timeline even began. He said we know so little of our true origins and of those who dwell on other worlds.

I started to relay the information as it came to me, "My guide said concerning the night tremors, as he calls them, that Lisa does not need to see a psychiatrist, and she does not need to be medicated. He said a pill will not address, nor cure the underlying cause of the night tremors. He stated she experiences these tremors in her sleep because of concern for her family. There is much worry and grieving by her over the actions taking place within the family and the negative energy being expressed. Do you understand what he is saying so far?" I asked trying not to sound judgmental.

Jody paused for a few seconds then responded, "Yes…your guide is right. Me and my husband have been arguing and fighting over the bills and I think he may have even cheated on me with another woman."

"He says there is a great need to create a harmonious, peaceful and loving environment within your home. He says though you may not feel Lisa is fully capable of understanding the complex intricacies of the world around her; there is much taking place that she sees, hears and is aware of, even subconsciously. She experiences these things because she is living in it with the rest of the family. She has no other way of expressing this conflict she observes and experiences; thus, it manifests itself as night tremors. Are you still following what he is saying?"

"Yes," her reply was simple, but I felt she wanted to ask a question but felt uncomfortable in doing so.

"Jody if you have anything you wish to ask please do so. There is no judgment from those on the other side, none what-so-ever." I tried to be positive and reassuring.

"So, what needs to be done then?"

"My guide says the elimination of certain aspects that are not a part of anyone's highest good should be acted upon. Know what is important for the harmony of the family unit. For Lisa he said to share time and love with her directly. No passive enjoyment from her; assist and guide her now. He says do not worry that she has been neglected in any way up to this point. Start anew with her right now or she will continue to experience these sleeping night tremors. If improvements are not made with the energy pattern of your current family situation, he says there will be a wearing down of her mind and therefore she will become accustomed to this negative energy which can have dire consequences for her later in life. The harmful effects of this prolonged negative energy will manifest in her future relationships and interactions with others she encounters. He says create peace and balance now within your family or this pattern will continue as it has through the previous generations."

"What does he mean through the previous generations?" Jody asked.

"He says you are the product of such a family unit that Lisa is now experiencing. Your parents were at great odds with each other and you as a child experienced night tremors yourself. That negative energy pattern that became a part of you is now affecting your compatibility with your spouse. If you do not break this pattern now, your daughter will grow up to..."

(Click) Jody hung up the phone. She never called again, but I did receive a $30 dollar check several days later in the mail. It contained only the check. I was hoping for some kind of explanation for the abrupt hang-up, but nothing was ever forthcoming.

I can only speculate on what had upset her so much that she felt inclined to stop the reading, but denial can be one way many try to deal with negative situations in our lives. It is not for me or anyone else to make a judgment against another.

You the reader can draw your own conclusions

concerning what happened.

Chapter Four

Andre Washington's wife, Eleanor called me to set up an appointment to receive a reading next Sunday afternoon concerning a dream her husband had experienced.

At the appointed time Mrs. Washington, absent her husband knocked on my apartment door; a very soft knock. She looked to be in her early seventies and was dressed modestly.

Answering the door, "I'm pleased to meet you, I'm Evelyn, please come in and make yourself comfortable."

After exchanging the usual pleasantries, I felt we were ready to proceed with the reading. She did not seem hurried or restless as some of those who come to me are inclined to be.

"You said on the phone your husband had a dream you wish to ask about, is that correct?"

"Yes, he had it last month. My husband is older than me and has always been afraid of dying. He won't visit anyone in the hospital; he won't go to funerals even if it is a family member or close friend. He will be coming up on his eighty-third birthday next month. You know how men are, he says it's nothing to dwell on, but I know better. Back in my forties I started reading about spiritualism and things of that nature. I know a lot of my friends think its hocus-pocus and con artists just out to take your money, but I know in my heart there's more to it then that.

They believe what they want, I believe what I

want, Amen." She was straight forward and

spoke softly.

"Can you tell me about the dream your

husband had experienced?"

"Yes ma'am, he says he wakes up and he is in a

hospital room. Everything is white; the walls, the

ceiling, the bed sheets and he's lying there in the

hospital bed, but he is not feeling any pain or

sickness and doesn't understand why he is there.

He says a nurse comes in wearing a white uniform

and comes over to his bedside with a big smile on

her cheery face. Andre asks her if he is alright.

The nurse takes his left hand in her left hand and

begins to pat the top of his hand with her other

had which he says makes him feel very loved and

comforted. She then answers his question by

saying everything is all right Mr. Washington,

you're dead, and she stands there smiling. After

she tells him he is dead my husband says he is not

afraid but feels great joy and love in his heart and

then he wakes up. I know in my heart he has had

this dream more than once, but he won't talk about

it and told me not to bring it up again. So, I come

here to see what meaning this dream is bringing to

him."

"Alright then, let me see what my guide has to

say about this dream." I relaxed and took a deep

breath. Alexander was already sending the

answer to me before I exhaled. "Those spirit companions who watch over Andre know of his fear of death and dying and they have been implanting, so to speak these dreams into his subconscious mind for several months now. So that when he does cross over to the unseen world, he will not be traumatized by his death experience. They are bringing these dreams now because his time of crossing over is drawing near and they wish for him to be more prepared when it comes time for his soul to leave his physical body. If he is in a more understanding frame of mind and not so fearful it will make the transition from the physical world to the spirit world go much easier for his soul, his true self. My guide is asking if you have another question."

There was a short pause before Eleanor spoke, "Will his death be quick or long and drawn out by sickness?"

"My guide says it will be a short and easy departure for him. The hardest part for him will be his misunderstanding that he is leaving you behind and will never see you again; which is not true. Once he becomes acclimated back into his true home world, he will then realize how much closer he is too you at that time; rather then to how separated you two are in the physical world of earth. That will be a great relief to him when he comes to that realization." I explained.

"How long before this happens?" She asked in a low fearful voice.

"According to my guide Andre has only weeks before its time for him to return." I said straight forward. "He says he will not give an exact date and time so as not to put that stress and worry into your mind."

"So how long before I can cross over and be with him in the spirit world? My children and grand children are all moved away to other states and we rarely get to see them. Am I destined to be alone for the rest of my days? (She began to cry) I truly don't think I could stand living without my beloved Andre."

Handing her some tissues, "May I ask how old you are Eleanor?" I made the request to see if Alexander could give me a time frame for the question she just asked.

"I'll be seventy-two on my next birthday." She had stopped crying for now.

Alexander was sending me his answer as she answered, "My guide says you still have a mission so-to-speak to complete on the earth plane and that you will be here until it is completed."

She began to plead, "What mission? Why can't Andre stay with me until this mission is done? He's always been the one to make the important decisions in our life together; I don't know what to do. I'm already afraid; I don't understand this new world we live in; all these fancy gadgets and machines. I can't work a computer or one of those new-fangled phones. Andre takes care of all that stuff. What am I to do? Please don't take my husband. We need more time together…" She burst out into tears!

Eleanor leaned over toward me and I wrapped my arms around her. I held her tightly as we both now cried together. I truly felt so sorry for this elderly woman, and I didn't know what to do for her. My emotional feelings changed my vibrational level and I lost my connection to Alexander. It took several minutes for us both to regain some of our composure.

Finally, after much nose blowing and almost a half box of tissue, we each, one after the other, retired to the bathroom to wash our faces, fix our make-up and whatnot. Sitting quietly on the sofa again I told her I was going to see if I could reconnect with my guide and see if we couldn't get more information on her future situation.

Relaxing, I did my deep breathing exercise which helps me mentally, physically and emotionally to tune back into the other side. Now I felt I was ready to make the connection again to the unseen world where Alexander patiently awaited. In an instant his thought came to me asking if I was ready to resume, and I most definitely was ready to seek some guidance to help this beautiful woman sitting nervously by my side.

Taking her hand in mine to reassure us both the communication came forth from Alexander, "My guide says that Andre cannot stay because it is his chosen time to depart. He has experienced and learned or not learned all that he came for, so now he is finished with this lifetime. He says that you have allowed Andre to make all the important decisions concerning your lives together and now as he departs it is time for you to come to the forefront and make decisions for yourself. You are stronger than you realize and are very capable of directing your life from this point forward. Do not fear for your spirit companion will always be with you when you need help or assistance now and in the future. So, you are not alone, and you may call upon Andre and he will send you comforting thoughts to help you through your remaining years on this planet..."

Eleanor interjected, "Years? How many years will I be here for?"

"He says your mission will keep you in a physical body for a little over...twenty more years." I was hesitant to answer at first not knowing how she would take this news, but if Alexander gives it to me then I figure the person it is for can handle it. I never censor what information comes through even if it seems negative; for there may be more to it then I myself realize since I cannot see what they can in the unseen world.

As her jaw dropped open, she sat staring in disbelief. A few moments later she uttered loudly, "Oh my God!"

Alexander continued, "He says he knows this is a lot for you to take in and he wants to stop for now so that you can have time to digest all that has been spoken here. He wants you to make arrangements to return in sixty days after you have had time to think and dwell upon all that has been presented to you. Then at the next reading he will explain the mission you are to undertake which will take almost twenty years to complete. This is a very important mission and you were

specifically chosen for it. You agreed to it
before you were born into this life; for up to now
he says you have only been 'existing' in this
lifetime, but now you are going to truly become
alive and give this lifetime true meaning."

Alexander withdrew at this point and the
communication stopped. Eleanor and I made
plans to meet up again in sixty days time to
further explore her 'mission' that was brought up
by Alexander.

My desire was that it would give her a glimmer
of hope for the future to know she was chosen for
a special mission, but she seemed overwhelmed
by all that was said concerning Andre and her
limited time remaining with her husband. If I

were in her shoes, I guess I too would be fearful

of facing the unknown future by myself, without

my loving companion by my side.

(Two months later)

Much had taken place since I last met with

Eleanor Washington. She had telephoned to

confirm her reading day and time earlier in the

week. I could feel the loneliness in her soft voice.

We spoke briefly on the phone and she said her

husband Andre had passed quietly in his sleep two

and a half weeks after our first reading. Most of

her children, two sons and three daughters and

their families flew in early to help with the funeral

arrangements and the like; only her youngest daughter Abigail couldn't be located.

Eleanor said it was wonderful to reunite with her children and grand children even during this time of sorrow in her life. All had to leave after the funeral to return to their hectic lives in other states; which she said she understood, but that brought on a slight depression and feelings of isolation she said.

Yet, overall, she was coming to terms with her new life; she had a neighbor who was helping her with all the new financial responsibilities and things of that nature. Mastering new things also brings with it a certain comfort or feeling of improved self worth which she had not experienced before. She said it was like a freedom she never new existed and that it was a truly wonderful feeling of empowerment.

Eleanor arrived early and I invited her in. We got settled in; both of us sitting in the same spots on the sofa as we had done on our last visit together. I had already prepared myself and was quietly awaiting her arrival, so I was ready to begin. She said she too was ready, so no chit-chat was necessary at this point.

Mentally I asked about her mission that had been spoken of at our last encounter. Alexander jumped right in with sending me the requested information, so I began to relay it to Eleanor.

"My guide says there is a very special child that will be coming into your life very soon. Your mission is to raise this child and provide it with love and compassion."

"What? I...I can't raise no more children. I'm an old woman now. I don't have the strength for something like that." She gasped and sighed heavily.

"My guide says you do have the strength for this important mission and your spirit companion, that which you call your Guardian Angel will be assisting you. Your so-called Angel will infuse you with healing energy daily so you will have the needed physical and mental strength for this task. When you are unsure of what to do simply close your eyes and mentally ask your Angel for

guidance. He will send you the thought that will

answer your question. Go with the first thought

that comes into your mind for that will be from

your Angel. Take action on that first thought, do

not sit and second guess or keep repeating your

question; for if you do, then your own mind will

interfere and cause doubt and try to sway you to

another course of action, which will be wrong

action. Many times, a person's mind well choose

fear over love, so do not be swayed. Have

confidence, over time you will know when your

Angel is guiding your thoughts and simply follow

them. He says when doubt enters your mind

simply release it and think of something beautiful, something pleasant. Do you understand so far?"

"Ah…yes, I'm following what you're saying, but where will this child come from? How old will it be...is it a baby? Is it a boy or a girl?" She now had many questions on her mind that needed answered and Alexander was ready for them.

"My guide says not to worry; all your important questions will be answered within a few days time."

This wasn't what Eleanor wanted to hear; you could almost feel the desperation coming from within her, "So there's nothing your guide can tell me about this child right now?"

"He says you will know what to do when it comes, your soul has been eagerly awaiting the arrival of this special child all these many years. Your mission is to raise this child with unconditional love. With compassion and joy you are to fill this special child with the understanding that all creatures in nature are a part of God and are to be treated with kindness and love just as all humans are to be treated the same. You will give this child no religious instruction of any kind; religion is not to be pushed or forced upon this child. It will follow its own path in this lifetime, and it will choose what it will believe or not believe while on its chosen journey. This child will not attend what you would call normal or regular school. You are to home school this child. Those of the unseen world as some term it does not wish this child to be exposed to the traditional schooling of this country due to its misguided representations of the factual truth of the world at large. This child will have an ability to communicate with its spirit companion as it grows to adulthood. When this child tells you of its 'so-called' imaginary friend just know it is not someone the child has invented in its mind to play with. This will be a spirit guide that will come in a form that will be in harmony with this child so as not to frighten; it will be seen as another child. As this child grows so will the appearance of the spirit guide change to mirror the age of this special soul. This spirit companion will be teaching universal spiritual truths and the laws of nature to this special being as it grows and will remain with it from birth until it returns to its true home."

Eleanor broke in, "What am I supposed to teach this child? What subjects; I haven't been to school for over fifty years or so. I..."

Alexander told me to interrupt her thought pattern and convey this to her, "My guide says you may go to the nearest school system and they will register the child as a home school individual and they will provide what the state requires to be taught. Do not fear; when these types of troubling thoughts arise simply sit quietly, close your eyes and mentally ask your Angel for help and in a short time you will receive the needed assistance. He also says to tell you that as the child grows his spirit companion will tell the child to tell you what is needed. The child may not understand the information he gives you, but you will understand and then will act upon it accordingly. Do not concern yourself with the child's education; its spirit companion will teach it of the true world and assist it with its homework assignments required by the school system. He says to take the child to the playground at the park and let it interact with other children. Let it see nature and Gods beauty for it will grow up normally. It will have many questions which it will discuss with its 'imaginary' friend, but it will seek its love and affection from you. Hugs and kisses and laughter you two will experience together. You will find a new love of life in your heart as you two explore new adventures together. As the child explores its new world you will rediscover the joy and serenity you felt were lost to you many years ago. Never fear again, for you have your Angel standing right behind you and behind your Angel stands God; who would dare stand against you! So be not afraid for you are watched over and protected always." This seemed to calm Eleanor down quite a bit. She seemed more relaxed and more at ease, at least for now.

"Why is this child so special?" She asked hesitantly not truly expecting an answer.

No answer was forth coming from Alexander, but then I felt a vibrational change from within. Alexander was no longer in tune with me. Another spirit being had come forward and over shadowed Alexander. I felt as if this other being was much more enlightened, more spiritually advanced then my guide. I could not see him in my mind as I do Alexander. This spirit came to me almost as an intense glowing white light; yet expressing and radiating pure love. I felt humbled to be in its presence. The decision seemed to have been made by that great being that Eleanor's last question could and should be answered. As this divine being now communicated to me its thoughts I felt so at peace within myself; words cannot describe how I felt on all levels; physically, mentally and emotionally.

As I was about to open myself to its message it simply placed me in a trance state and used my form to convey its message directly to Eleanor, which I completely allowed as it asked my permission to do so. I heard these words come forth, "This soul has returned to earth to help usher in a new type of peace that was lost to this world centuries ago. This great soul shall draw thousands of lost souls to it who will be desperately seeking to find their way out of the darkness of this misguided world. Much darkness shall befall this world in the future and souls of this kind are now incarnating to be of great service to humankind in those times of great sorrow. Mankind has brought this destruction upon itself and now must learn a most severe lesson." I felt this great presence move slowly away as I was released from the trance state, I had been placed in. I was now aware of Alexander's presence.

"Oh, my goodness." Was all Eleanor could say.

Alexander then withdrew and the reading was now closed. Eleanor and I shared some tea and discussed her message for a short time before she had to leave. She said she would keep in touch as she departed. I now sat quietly and contemplated on the 'destruction' that the advanced spirit had

mentioned was coming in the future.

(Seven months later)

Drying myself off after a most refreshing bath

I heard the faint ringing of my telephone.

Dressing quickly into my bathrobe I scurried into

the living room, but the caller had already hung

up. Checking the Caller-ID display I dialed the

number; to my delight it was Eleanor who

answered in her sweet voice.

She gave me an update on what had happened

since our last reading. A young man carrying a

small red gym bag came knocking on her door

late one evening. He looked to be in his early to

middle twenties she stated. Peeking out the window she was afraid to open the door to this stranger. As this man kept knocking, he noticed her looking out the window. Placing the red gym bag down in front of her door she said he seemed to be writing something on a piece of paper. Then he pointed to the bag with his right hand and then turned and drove off in an old black Honda Civic.

She watched for a few minutes before opening her front door. There was a folded-up note lying on top of the gym bag. Opening her door, she reached down to retrieve the note when she heard the baby inside the gym bag crying. She said she new immediately that this was the special child she was to care for and raise.

After bringing the bag and note inside she removed the infant and discovered it was a boy and began to mother it; soothing it and caring for it. Eleanor said she had already bought diapers, formula and all that would be needed in preparation of the arrival of the special child.

After it fed and finally fell asleep, she sat down to read the note. To her shock it said the baby was from her youngest daughter Abigail and that she had died just two days ago at the county hospital and that her unclaimed body is there now in the mortuary. The note further said the man could not care for the baby and explained that he was just a friend and not the baby's father. The note was unsigned.

Calls to the hospital said Abigail had been shot once in the left side of her face while sitting in a parked car. She never regained consciousness and died a short time later from the complications. Police have no suspects in the shooting at this time. Police think it may have been drug related Eleanor said.

She called the family, and all came and helped her with the funeral arrangements. Some family members were surprised she said after telling them she was going to raise the infant; but all said for her to call if they were ever needed.

No birth certificate could be located so she got an attorney and established through the court system she was now his legal guardian and said she was inspired in a dream to name him 'Martin Luther Washington.'

After that call we would have no further contact. There were times later in my life that I had wished I had stayed in touch with this wonderful woman. But, like so many others I was caught up in the rat race of my personal life and missed the opportunity of what could have been an endearing friendship.

* Note to Reader: Concerning Andre's returning home; spiritually speaking death is like opening a door and walking through it. There you find yourself back at your true home; with true friends, companions and family who rejoice at your

return. You completed that lifetime; learning and experiencing as much as you could or couldn't. Later, you will be waiting to greet those loved ones you left behind on earth when they have finished their lifetime and they cross over. You will rejoice with them at their special reunion.

Yes, many people fear death because of their religious faith and/or upbringing. They fear the 'Hell' that was programmed into them by their misguided religious beliefs. Religion told them they 'Sinned against God' and therefore they must be damned to a burning 'Hell' with Satan torturing them throughout eternity. But once their soul crosses over and they are met by their friends and loved ones they soon realize no one is there to

judge them or to send them to hell. They then

realize that Hell and Satan and all the other

negative things; were just made up devices to

control them while living in a human form on the

earth plane. Religions and governments on the

earth use various means to control the people they

hold influence over. Most times it is of a negative

type of control.

Humankind created religions, not God. The

'Source of all Life' as God is called in the spirit

world loves all of his creations unconditionally.

When you return home to the spirit world, he does

not judge you for what you did or did not do on

the earth. You will review that lifetime and

decide whether you did or did not accomplish

certain lessons and then with higher guidance you

will plan your next journey of discovery. No

punishment of any kind will be placed upon you.

The negative events you experienced, or you

created while upon the earth were simply for

learning and spiritual growth; that of yourself and

that of humankind.

Chapter Five

My friend, Winston Thomas who is a trance medium invited me and several other close friends over for a séance. This was held in his basement. We were given the option of receiving a 'Past Life' reading or a 'Future Life' reading. Winston's spirit guide who will be speaking through him is known as Dr. George Wilson.

Dr. Wilson: Yes, this is Dr. George Wilson. I'm the spirit companion or what some my term guardian angel for this instrument. Greetings, my understanding is that some may be interested in past or future lifetimes. I have looked into this for those who are present here tonight.

We will be working under a time restraint this evening due to the physical limitations of the instrument. Therefore, in order to accommodate everyone gathered some may feel as though their reading may be a little short, and I do apologize for this in advance.

Now at this time I wish to give you each a choice, and I want you to simply see before you two doors. The door on the left will be the door to a past life. The door on your right will be the door that opens to your next physical existence in the earth plane. I will give you your choice of choosing whether you wish to have discussed a past life or the life that you will live the next time you incarnate into the physical body of a human. This will be your choice you see. Now did everyone understand what I said.

Group: Yes.

Dr. Wilson: Alright then, Keith, do you wish to go first?

Keith: Yes.

Dr. Wilson: Which door do you choose Keith?

Keith: The right door.

Dr. Wilson: Now, I want you all to understand that there is a spiritual law that I will be working under and I'll explain it to you. The law is that I will not always give you a date, and I want to explain that. If I were to say, for example; in the year 2037 you were going to be born and do this and that. Then when you reach a certain age in this life, you may say, 'Hey, I've got to die in order to get over there in time to get everything ready for my next life.'

You see, so I don't want that. So, I will not give you certain dates. I wish it not to be in your subconscious mind. Everyone understands if you pick the door to your right, I will withhold the date because your subconscious mind will cause you concern and worry and a lot of wasted effort in thought.

However, I will tell you that being in your subconscious, any information that is given to you while in the physical state will be most difficult to erase after you have been reincarnated. Do you understand?

You will have more recall then at the actual time of birth. The spirit itself is being instructed into its earth life before birth. Do you understand?

Keith: No.

Mayme: If you're born again Keith, you will remember what he's telling you now.

Dr. Wilson: Yes, because you are being given the information now, while you are in a human form; you will recall it in the next life. You will have more recall; you will remember what takes place here tonight. Understand?

Keith: I think so.

Dr. Wilson: When you are living that future life, if I say on a particular day a certain thing will happen, you will have total recall and say, "Well I was looking forward to it happening."

Keith: Okay, I understand now.

Dr. Wilson: Good, very well. Of course, for those who choose the door on the left, the recall will not have a plus or minus for you.

Jane: I have a question, if you choose the left door, are you going to give dates?

Dr. Wilson: Yes, dates are always given in past life readings with only a few exceptions.

Jane: Oh...okay, I didn't know.

Dr. Wilson: This knowledge will be coming from the Akashic Records. It might be called the

Higher Hall of Records. It has many names, or it means many different things to many different people. It is the Higher Hall of Akashic Records when the future life is there.

Now I will begin with you Keith. If you have questions, feel free at any time to ask. This is Dr. George Wilson; I will be working tonight.

Keith: Okay.

Dr. Wilson: In your future life, the life that is already planned, the life that has been laid out, the life that you are working towards now; that you are obtaining knowledge and information and being guided towards. I will now begin. I will turn the page of the book and I will start with the very beginning of the time of birth.

This may seem insignificant to you tonight but in the next life it will mean a great deal. It will mean a great deal to people who study the stars and the planets. So, the time will be important to them and to you.

You will be born the Earth time of 6:03am. It will be a Thursday. Your mother will end her physical existence at 6:08am, Thursday.

You will be raised in a home that is not unlike the homes of today of an orphanage, but it will be called more of a training institution.

Your father will not reject you, if you're wondering why the institution, your father will not reject you, but it will be the way of the time that you have been born in.

Your father will be a man in the service of the government in the way of, not a politician, but as a keeper of peace. You may in your lifetime, this lifetime that you are living in now call the gentleman a career soldier. But he will be a gentleman of peace instead of this other term.

I will reveal to you at this time the names of those people. Your name will be…now this is no pun. Your name will be exactly the same as your first now, but it will be spelled backwards; Htiek. Do you understand so far?

Keith: Yes.

Dr. Wilson: Very good. Your mother, whom you will never know, will be named 'Navarone.' Your father's name will be 'Harmzes.' The last name, the family name of your family will be 'Eiruman.'

Now then, through the institutional care and through the studies and the schooling, you will go into the scientific study of planetary study. This will be normal study for that time.

You will spend your career not upon this planet. Your life basically will be a dweller of space. You will be traveling from one area to another. Much similar to the airlines of today, which go from one city to another city or from one continent to another continent. But this will be of a more colorful, advanced type of flight which will take place out in space. More like going from one planet to another planet.

You will never marry. You will perish and return to the spiritual dimension after a period of earth years numbering forty-seven. I will not disclose the nature of the death, for it will have no bearing upon this life when you do recall. You will be in another dimension. You will be in another galaxy, and you will perish. But know that you shall be as close to spirit then as you are now. There will be no reason to fear being lost there in a vast nothingness, because it is not a vast nothingness.

Keith: Will I have the same feelings and emotions as I have now?

Dr. Wilson: No. You're going to be developed as a scientist. You will have no emotion. You will have feeling. You will not have emotions; you have primitive emotions now. You will not have emotions in the future life. This is Dr. George Wilson.

Keith: Ah, thank you.

Dr. Wilson: All right Renesha, which door would you like to choose?

Renesha: I'll take the left one.

Dr. Wilson: In your past life, I'm going to skip with you and at a later date I'll go into your last existence.

I want to go back into time when you were what many people of today would call a monk. You were of the male sex. You spent a great deal of time in monastery work; which was primarily praying, gardening and teaching.

Renesha: Wait a second…you're saying I was a man?

Dr. Wilson: I shall explain for those who wish this knowledge. Your Soul or Spirit, whatever word you desire to use is simply made up of intelligent energy; the essence of this energy is a part of that which many call God or Great Spirit or Creator which is also intelligent energy.

As an energy being, you are part of God, you are not male or female but may then choose to be either when you incarnate into this physical plane where you must take on the mantle of male or female. Your race, your nationality, your parents, to be rich or poor and much more are chosen by you before your birth into this world. Are you following the pattern I am speaking of?

Renesha: Yes, I understand.

Dr. Wilson: Very well, now then, as a monk in that life you had reached a certain knowledge and degree of your own. You did not pass away due to old age. When the hoards of Genghis Khan came through your area, you were cut down, decapitated. You lost your head, your arms, your legs and were disemboweled.

Renesha: I was told by a psychic friend of mine that Genghis Khan was punished for what he did in that lifetime. Is that true?

Dr. Wilson: He was not punished for that lifetime, just as Adolf Hitler was not punished for the life he lived in Nazi Germany. But to balance the karmic debt incurred for the life he lived as Genghis Khan, he later reincarnated and lived that lifetime of the one known to many as Joseph Merrick the 'Elephant Man.'

Now then, to continue with your past life Renesha, upon entering the monastery he did not take the vow of silence because he was a teacher and instructor.

The name of the monk of this existence was Xavier but was of a different pronunciation. He went only by Xavier.

Now the date of passing, due to a new experience of another life that is to come, I wish not to divulge the date of death because of the horror of the death. The second of that death will carry over and into another life with a similar earth experience. I wish not to place the date of death because the date will correspond with the coming date of death.

That being the one that is important in mathematics in that lifetime, in that mathematical equation of death; she will find the answer, and it will cause much disturbance to her, so I will not divulge that date for her.

Renesha: So, I'm going to die the same way in this life as that one?

Dr. Wilson: No, not this life, but your future planned life you will be…I will be cruel with this, yes, in your future programmed life you will be murdered on the same month and day you were murdered during your past life we are discussing now. It will simply be a different date for the year, which will be far into the future as you count time. So, there is nothing to fear, simply new experiences of your own choosing. This is Dr. George Wilson.

Renesha: I get it, thanks.

* Note to Readers: Concerning Adolf Hitler, my guide Alexander said he was not judged or forced to punish himself but was to undergo a form of

counseling. Many of the actions, developments and forms of review he underwent upon his return to the spirit world were self-imposed. Alexander said it is possible, for any being, to accomplish such acts as were carried out in his lifetime and be unaware of the severity of their actions. Hitler was able to return, if he chose, and not fully become aware of the direct involvement and severity of his acts while in the human form. This being (Hitler) has made progress through counseling, through reviews, through reflection of the actions that were taken during that specific lifetime. It is in this process now that he currently finds himself and there is much progress being made. There were many things that were not reported through historical records or through media, or through the controlled outlets. There were many things that were taking place within this lifetime that lead to this series of events for many souls to undergo. It was not necessarily an evil act but an attempt to display the atrocities of the relating actions and ideals that brought forth this mentality into the physical world and lead to the violent death and actions taken in the name of the government who sanctioned and made right, true, or correct the actions of the people for the sake of power. It should be evidenced by historical document that there were no lasting positive outcomes that could have been brought about by acting in this manner; developing hatred, annihilation, theses are not useful. Yet the men and women of this planet regularly engage in them on some scale. This was the lifetime of Hitler to involve himself in these actions in this manner, though there was a great deal of external motivation and influence by those with whom he surrounded himself. For, it was not entirely his motivation alone that lead to the final outcome.

Dr. Wilson: Now Mayme, are you ready? Which door do you wish to open?

Mayme: The left.

Dr. Wilson: You wish to seek a past life experience. Very well, I'd like to place you at this time in the nation or country of Canada. I'm placing you there and giving you the name in which you will not enjoy. You have never in any life had a name you enjoyed. I wish to give you the name of your last, next to last incarnation. This is not the last one. This is the one before. The name that I give you is Malinda.

Mayme: It's better than the one I got now.

Dr. Wilson: Yes, but you didn't think so then.

Mayme: Probably not, it's not the prettiest.

Dr. Wilson: Now Mayme, like the 'M' is very important in your life to you. You feel closeness to the 'M', and I think it's because of the spirit god sound of 'OM.'

Now then, let us go along with this and you can see some of the character peculiarities coming out, because of the Canadian life and to this one. I skipped a life. It didn't show up in your last life that's the reason I picked the one before to speak on this evening.

This is why you are always hot. You like cool weather. You're cool natured. You like cool places. Many of your lives which have been few have been spent in cool areas on the earth.

Now, the family name of this one of which I'm speaking of was Sheller. You were not French. You were a Duke's mixture. You were English. Your parents came from England.

Now, Malinda Sheller was born in the year 1637. You were married and raised three children. You gave birth to seven children, four did not live. They had short life spans. Three

that survived lived to adulthood.

You were alone a lot in your life, for your

husband was an explorer type. He was working

for the government in bringing about mapping of

the land. He was exploring the land areas for the

leaders and officials of that time period.

You live to be the age of eighty-seven. So,

you may add your birth date to see the date you

died, passed away. You passed away in October

of that year, the 21st. The month of birth wasn't

as important as it would have been to Keith. It

was May 12th.

You had a great deal in common through that

experience with the Indians in that area. You

were not an Indian lover, but you tolerated the Indian people. You were no missionary by any means.

Mayme: What was my married name?

Dr. Wilson: Malinda Bonyea. He was French.

Mayme: Well, between this last life and the one in 1600 must have been a long time in between there.

Dr. Wilson: Yes, you needed a long period of development in the spiritual dimension. Now then, do you have another question about that period?

Mayme: Is that the reason I want to go to Canada now, because of that prior life?

Dr. Wilson: Yes.

Mayme: Where did I live?

Dr. Wilson: You were close to a large Indian village or encampment they called it. This is Dr. George Wilson.

Mayme: Oh…thank you.

Dr. Wilson: Now then, moving on, let's see…David are you ready?

David: The right one please.

Dr. Wilson: I would like to explain how it is arrived at a future existence, and it is the future life as programmed, so to speak, from your past experience. In many past lives you're being guided in a direction to be of future service in a coming life or experience. It is basically the same life; you are the same being, same soul. You are being placed in a different experience.

Now David, are you ready to open the door on your right?

David: Yes.

Dr. Wilson: Very well, again I will not be giving you dates or ages or years so as not to concern you dearly or deeply now.

In your next earth experience you will be female. You will be from a large family. The time and day of your birth I will give although it will again not carry the importance to you that Keith's will to him. Your birth will be 8:12pm on a Sunday. It will be raining. You will be in the country known as France.

As I spoke earlier, you will be of the female sex. You will have tremendous abilities as a child in the Arts.

You will not marry young, but you will marry; however, you will not produce children.

You will develop in your thirties a writing ability. You will write many volumes of knowledge on the Arts. You will develop a philosophy through your writings.

You will, for a time, live in seclusion during your periods of deep thought in your career.

In your twilight years of your life you will expand and broaden out in the field of appearing before audiences in speaking and lecturing.

Your passing will be normal. Everything goes according to the records as I see them, you should live to be eighty-one years old in your next earth existence, not this one.

Now then, the birth name of this child will be a strange name too. It will be Feon Monet Break. When she does marry, the married name of the gentleman she marries will be Marchant.

Do you have any questions?

David: No. Thank you.

Dr. Wilson: Now Evelyn, I have for you two doors, one on the left and one on the right. Which will be your pleasure?

Evelyn: Left.

Dr. Wilson: We open the door and enter into a room of a past life. In the past life that you have completed, you are seeking some verification. I will give you something here for you to puzzle over. You were not a doctor; you were one who worked as a doctor.

I am placing you right in the middle of the Revolutionary War in this country. You were not Martha Washington, yet you knew of her and some others. But your name, a common name, was JoAnne Wilcox.

Now there were three marriages. JoAnne Wilcox Circee was the first, JoAnne Wilcox Circee LaMarz was the second and the third was JoAnne Wilcox Circee LaMarz Blankenheimer and it was a Jewish name. Two of the gentlemen were killed in the war and the other one outlived you. Yes, you lost two close together.

You were close to much of the fighting at that time, which spread all over a great area. Most of your life though was spent in the Virginia region.

Now then, May 30th was the date of your birth. The year was 1741. In earth years you were going into your ninety-third birthday when you passed.

You were born in what the Indians called a wigwam...

Evelyn: I wasn't American?

Dr. Wilson: Yes, you were an American citizen.

Evelyn: You said I wasn't a doctor?

Dr. Wilson: You had a very limited nurse training, but you were called upon to do the acts that a doctor would do in a type of emergency. You did many midwife acts and you doctored many people. There were no doctors available many of the times in the areas where you were at, and you assumed the duties. You had a lot of courage. You liked to use or were adept at using a knife in the way of surgery.

Evelyn: Was this from a prior life?

Dr. Wilson: Yes, I feel as though you got your fill.

Evelyn: I used up all my courage (laughing).

Dr. Wilson: I will say this, in a prior life even before this one we're speaking of; you were a man. You were a brute. You did commit chaos and murder. You bludgeoned people to death with instruments of war.

So, in that life I am speaking of, the last one, the sight of blood and gore didn't annoy you.

Now you have come a long way because you have outgrown that. See the improvements and progressions you have made?

Evelyn: Yes.

Dr. Wilson: This is Dr. George Wilson.

Evelyn: Thank you very much.

Dr. Wilson: Now then, which door would you like to choose Michael?

Michael: The left one for a past life.

Dr. Wilson: I'm placing you in the nation or country of Italy. Now I wish not to divulge the name because he was born to a family of prestige in that era. You were very much at the forefront of a major religion; that is where you found your structure, your belief system, and in the end your demise. You were well known in your circles because of your dedication and pushing for release of information, and for release from oppression.

You were fighting for equality, for fairness and understanding for the people. Your past life was one of exile and persecution; dying at the hands of those with differing world views from your own.

You had been assigned a personal quest in that lifetime and because of this you did not give up your beliefs or change for the sake of a better life outside of imprisonment.

Michael: So, I died in prison?

Dr. Wilson: You were being held by the religious organization. Through torture and imprisonment, they were trying to force you to stop speaking out against the oppression and control they were exerting upon the people who followed this major religion.

When they saw that you would not be swayed, they decided to end your existence through the avenue of murder.

Michael: How old was I when they murdered me?

Dr. Wilson: You were forty-three. All of your previous lifetimes, with the exception of two have been short lifetimes.

This is Dr. George Wilson. God's blessings upon this gathering.

End

Chapter Six

It had been almost two years since I last did a reading for my old friend from high school. Bonnie Sue Anderson is a forty-two-year-old mother of a beautiful little eight-year-old named Jenny; her only child. Her husband is named Jason and they all live in southern California in a large ranch style home.

Bonnie Sue and family had flown to Florida due to the death of her husbands' uncle. After the funeral she called the next day and asked if we could get together and also if she could get a reading. I was delighted and looked forward to her arrival the next morning.

She came alone, leaving her husband and daughter to get acquainted with some of the relatives that never had the opportunity to meet Jenny before.

We reminisced a little about the old days and talked about what had been going on for the last two years since we last saw each other. It wasn't long before she broached the subject of a reading and I was most happy to accommodate her.

"So, would you like just a simple reading, or do you have something specific you wish to ask about?" I began.

"I have been having dreams that all seem to have the same basic theme to them. I just want some clarity." Bonnie Sue stated in a straightforward manner.

"Okay, tell me about the last dream." I closed my eyes and started my deep breathing exercise relaxing myself for Alexander's arrival.

"My dreams all revolve around my older brother Karl. In my dreams it is made known to me that he has a brain tumor and is going to die. I saw him not long ago and he is in perfect health. So, I wanted some kind of confirmation before I tell him of the dreams I'm having. I don't want to alarm him, but if he has a brain tumor, he needs to see a specialist as soon as possible." You could hear the love and emotion in her voice.

"Alright, my guide is saying the dreams you are having have nothing to do with your brother Karl. He, nor you have a brain tumor. These dreams are for you. There will be much loss around you, and you will view this as devastation and traumatic. Your spirit companion has been sending these dreams to your subconscious in order to prepare you for the coming tragedy that will unfold in your near future. Your spirit companion is using your dreams to prepare you because he has no other way to instill this message to you. He says you have a strong psychic ability, yet you have relinquished all interest and use for it. You are very much involved in the material side of life; the buying and gathering of things which have no true worth. Material things do not bring true happiness, they only offer misguided hope to those seeking to foster love in their empty lives. A change in your thinking about this future event now will prepare you to deal with the fallout that will occur afterward. He is saying you need to prepare now, prepare your mind and thoughts so you are mentally and emotionally ready to make the necessary decisions at the time of the impending tragedy."

"What tragedy?" She asked hesitantly.

"My guide says you already know the answer to that question. That you have already discussed this with your husband." I must admit I was curious to know what the tragedy was, but if Alexander didn't tell me then it wasn't for me to know.

After a short pause, "Yes, your guide is correct. I do know what he is referring to. Can he tell me when this may come about?"

"Within the next three-year period as he see's it in our understanding of time."

"Will there be financial help available to me after that event?"

"My guide says there will be almost no financial help available to you at that point in time. Your world as you now know it will crumble and disappear. You will have two paths placed in front of you; one leading to a new way of life and one leading into darkness as he see's it. You will have the free will to choose which path you will walk for your remaining days upon this planet." As I brought forth that information Bonnie Sue began to cry.

Through her tears she asked, "Is there nothing I can do to stop it before it happens?"

Alexander seemed to pause before he sent me the answer, "No." That was all he gave me and that was all I conveyed to Bonnie Sue as I felt Alexander withdraw from my vibration.

She excused herself to my bathroom and after emerging she said she needed to get back to her family. They would be flying back to California in the early morning. We hugged and I wished her well and gave my condolences on her husbands' family loss. I would never hear from her again in this lifetime.

(Seven years later)

It had been a long day for me. I was mentally and physically tired. Preparing to enter a hot bath I had just made the phone started ringing. I decided to ignore it and would call whoever it was back tomorrow.

As I was disrobing Alexander popped in and said, "Evelyn, please answer the phone. It is important." I was a little caught off guard for Alexander had never done this before; I always made first contact so to speak.

Putting my robe back on I headed into the living room. To my amazement the phone was still ringing. Answering, it was Karl Anderson, Bonnie Sue's brother. I had only new him from our old high school days and had not seen or heard from him since that time. We were never close as they say; he was two years ahead of us in school, so he wasn't in our 'click' of friends so to speak.

Karl said he wasn't sure why he felt the need to call me; for some unknown reason my name just popped into his head and he's been thinking about me for over a week. He said he felt compelled to look me up and he finally gave in and called.

We had a very short phone conversation before I asked how his sister Bonnie Sue was doing. There was surprise in his voice for he had thought his sister had surely called and told me of the events that had taken place. He then told me of the tragedy that had befallen the family four years ago, three years after the reading I had given her.

Jason Anderson her husband had just received a plaque in recognition of his outstanding work achievement at his place of employment; manager of the year it read. After the presentation Karl said there was a staff party. During the celebration it was noticed Jason was missing and several employees went in search of their boss and friend.

Jason was found dead in his car in the parking lot. He had shot himself in the head with a revolver. Beside him on a notepad he had simply written; 'It's time for me to return home my love. I look forward to seeing you in the next world. Please explain to Jenny and give her my love.'

All employees questioned by police said he seemed very much in good spirits after the ceremony and said the same concerning the party afterward.

Karl said his sister's life deteriorated rapidly over the following year. Bonnie Sue told him and the other family members how they were hiding from everyone the fact that they were very much in financial debt. They had two mortgages on their home; their credit cards were almost maxed out. They were having trouble paying their monthly car payments and the list went on and on. They didn't want anyone to know how they were robbing 'Peter-to-pay-Paul' he said.

Bonnie Sue had confided in Karl after Jason's death that he had been very depressed and was seeing a psychiatrist who had him on medication. But the medication only seemed to dull his mind and added to his mental and emotional problems she told Karl. Toward the end they could no longer afford the doctor visits so that was stopped.

It had gotten so bad that Bonnie Sue had told Jason if he was thinking of suicide, he had better not kill himself in the house. She did not want their daughter finding his body. Jason said if it came to that, he would comply with her wishes Karl said.

There was a small company insurance policy used for funeral expenses, but it did not cover all the costs. They had already used Jason's 401k money and cashed in their life insurance policies trying to stave off the mounting debt. They were trying to live the lifestyle of the American dream Karl said, but Bonnie Sue told him that dream could no longer be maintained.

The house went into foreclosure and they were forced out; her and her daughter. Jason's parents were already living on their meager social security so they could offer no assistance. Bonnie Sue's parents had already passed on. Karl said they stayed with him for a short while.

He said her so-called friends all gave good lip-service at the funeral, but none could spare a dime or any personal time to help her or her daughter when they truly needed it. Maybe they too were all striving for the great American dream but were secretly struggling just as Bonnie Sue and Jason were. I try not to judge for who truly knows what lessons other people are facing in their personal lives.

Karl said Bonnie Sue was very depressed for almost a year over losing her husband, losing her lifestyle, losing her so-called friends and losing her self-identity. All her material things; house, furnishings and even some treasured personal items had to be sold to help pay debts. Both cars were repossessed. She had to declare bankruptcy. A small one-bedroom apartment was all she could afford for herself and her daughter Jenny.

He went on to say that his sister spiraled down the dark path of alcoholism, which he felt was brought on by the severe depression she had succumbed to. She was fired from her job because of the complications arising from her drinking problem.

Bonnie Sue was shortly thereafter committed to a State Facility after she tried to commit suicide by mixing old prescriptions with vodka. Jenny found her unconscious and called Uncle Karl because she didn't know what to do. He called 911. Family services became involved.

Karl said he stepped in at that point and moved Jenny in with him to keep her out of foster care. Jenny was an emotional mess and was assigned to see a school counselor twice a week.

Bonnie Sue had been placed on a suicide watch at the facility. She refused to eat and only kept stating she wanted to go back home. When her psychiatrist asked her where home was; she repeatedly said she was from another dimension.

She kept asking that her body be destroyed so she could free her spirit from this world. That brought on strong medication and forced intravenous feeding from her Doctor's he said. I felt so sad for her and Jenny I was softly crying as Karl continued on with their saga.

Then something miraculous happened on the seventeenth day of her confinement; she sat up in her bed and said she wanted to see the man-in-charge of her care. The head psychiatrist was summoned, and she told him she no longer wished to die, but now wanted to live. She began to eat on her own, to exercise, showing interest in everything and everyone she came in contact with. Months later she was released from the facility with a new lease on life as it were.

During her confinement Karl felt it would be better if he and Jenny had no contact with her; which had come at the behest of her attending Doctor. At first, Bonnie Sue who was now only going by the name 'Sue' made no attempts to contact her daughter or her brother. She found employment in the healthcare system and established a residence in a lower-middle class area of southern California.

To his great surprise a close friend of his said she had attended a psychic fair held by a local spiritualist group and that Sue was there giving psychic readings.

After not hearing from Sue for almost a year Karl decided it was time to see what Sue's intentions were toward Jenny. Karl's friend alerted him to the next upcoming psychic fair which was four months later. The fair was being held at a Holiday Inn on a Saturday and Sunday only. Arriving mid-morning he entered the large room and saw that Sue was sitting at a small fold-out card table, as were five other psychic's giving readings at separate card tables.

Paying for a reading he awaited his time slot and approached the small table and sat down across from her. She greeted him as if she had never laid eyes on him before. Stunned, he sat quietly as she started to give him a reading.

Abruptly she stopped and asked Karl if they had been acquainted in some fashion.

Not knowing what to believe he began to explain who he was; about her husbands' suicide and the events that had led her down the road to attempting suicide herself, and that she had a daughter who loved and missed her very much. She told him she had vague memories of the things and events he now spoke of but did not feel any connection; mental or emotional to him or Jenny.

He asked her about this new psychic ability she now alleged to have. Sue said not long after leaving the facility she woke up one morning and just knew she had the ability, and she started

using it. It was just so natural she said.

No further contact was forthcoming on his part

he said. He provided her with his phone number

and home address if she changed her mind and

wished to have contact with him or her daughter.

After all this time Sue has made no attempts to

contact either of them, he said sadly.

Karl then asked if I could give him a reading

over the phone. As I was about to explain how

tired and exhausted, I was, hoping we could

schedule it for another time I suddenly felt energy

surging into my body. No longer did I feel

mentally, emotionally or physically tired. It was

as if I had gotten eight hours of refreshing sleep.

Knowing Alexander was behind this I told Karl

to give me a few minutes to prepare myself and I

would be glad to read for him.

"Okay Karl, what would you like to ask first?"

"Was it the depression and drinking or was it

the strong medications they were giving her at the

state hospital that caused her overall memory

loss?" His tone not only conveyed confusion but a

hint of anger.

"Alright, my…"

"How could she not remember us…especially

her own daughter?!" I could hear the negative

emotion attached to his words; the anger and

frustration of what had played out over the last several years.

"Karl?"

There was a short pause, "Yes, I'm here. Sorry, I'm just so bewildered by all this."

"Take a deep breath and let me see what my guide has to say about all this. Can you do that for me?" My tone was soft and reassuring.

"Sure, I can do that." His voice was no longer angry but came across as simply tired and stressed.

"My guide is saying this may be hard to understand at first, but later once you think on it, you will come to a better understanding of what he is going to explain to you now. Your sister

Bonnie Sue had reached a point where she felt she could not continue in this lifetime. During her attempted suicide while she was unconscious her spirit companion, along with a highly advanced spiritual being, allowed her soul to leave her physical body so that it could be counseled. At that time, it was determined that her soul could not continue on at which point it asked to be allowed to return to the world of spirit. The higher advanced spirit after communicating with her spirit companion gave approval. Her soul was released from the body and another soul (walk-in) agreed to take over her body in order to fulfill its own personal set of lessons it was working on. My guide says that is why the one now known as

Sue has only a vague remembrance of you and

Jenny. Do you understand so far?"

There was a long pause before Karl spoke,

"Are you kidding me? What are you trying to

feed me? One soul taking over another soul's

body...what a bunch of fuckin' bullshit! You

know, I never liked you and I told Bonnie Sue to

stay away from crazy people like you. Go sell

your voodoo shit somewhere else." After his

abrupt hang-up, I never heard from him again.

* Note to Readers: From a Spiritual standpoint

suicide is no different an exit from earth then any

other manner of death. This, as others, is a

physical action manifested from the thoughts and

stress that persist on a person's mind. These can be overcome in the physical, and if not, there are many counseling sessions and advisements when that soul returns to the spirit world so that they can understand what torment they felt they were experiencing. Often times, those who commit suicide are young souls; those who have not yet had many life experiences in a physical form, and this is something they must overcome in order to continue learning in the lifetimes through the human form. Young souls who no longer remember their true home world become confused by being trapped in a human body and desperately seek to escape from their perceived confinement on a subconscious level. Committing suicide is no more or less negative or positive than any other action taken on the earth plane. Self-inflected death only returns a soul back to the spirit world; just as dying from old age, a disease or even murder or war accomplish the same. There is no judgment from God for a Soul to exercise its free will. Once a soul has been counseled and it decides it is ready, it will incarnate again into human form facing those same conditions with the desire to overcome them and grow spiritually. There are times when suicide is not only for the individual committing it but may simply be a lesson for those family and/or friends who are associated with the person committing this act. In that instance it becomes a matter of restoring love; you have seen family's

that seem to be scattered yet when such a

perceived tragedy occurs, they come together

again; re-establishing their love and commitment

for each other. Suicide can be a lesson in its own

right; not just the act of a seemingly desperate

individual.

Chapter Seven

Mark and Linda Goldman live in the apartment down the hall from mine. We have exchanged pleasantries passing in the hallway but nothing more. They seem like a nice young Jewish couple who have a beautiful one-year old baby boy named Davin.

Several days ago, the Goldman's discovered their son had died in his sleep and the authorities had ruled it a 'Crib Death.' Needless to say, they were very distraught and devastated at this event. Both husband and wife fell into deep depressions; the mother more so than the father.

As they struggled in the following months to reclaim their lives; one could say 'time' does heal all deep emotional wounds, but it does so slowly.

I was in the community laundry room washing two loads of clothes when Linda Goldman came in carrying a basket full of dirty clothes. She gave a short, half-hearted attempt at smiling as she passed by me and headed to the end washing machine. Returning her smile with a nod of acknowledgement I went back to a romance novel I had been reading while waiting for the spinning cycle to finish.

Looking up from my paper back novel I then noticed the elegant older woman, who was holding a small infant standing just several feet from where Linda was now sitting. My psychic ability told me immediately this regal woman was her grandmother and the infant were her son who had died from 'Sudden Infant Death Syndrome.'

From past experience I knew her grandmother wanted to make contact with her bereaved granddaughter, yet once again I wasn't sure how to initiate the communication between the two. Summoning my courage, I got up and sat down in the chair next to Linda Goldman. She was just staring at the floor.

"I'm sorry to bother you, I'm Evelyn Adams and I live down the hall from you in apartment forty-nine."

Linda broke off her intense stare and turned toward me. "Are you speaking to me?"

"Yes, I'm Evelyn…"

"What do you want?" Linda was very direct and plainly didn't want to be disturbed.

"I'm sorry for my intrusion but I just wanted to offer my condolences on the passing of your son."

After a long blank stare, she finally spoke, "You have never said more then two words to me or my husband since we moved in. Now after all this time you now dare to offer your condolences on the tragic death of our son. You think I don't know who you are? People in the building talk about you…you're nothing more than a fortune teller who prays on the weak minded. You need to get away from me before I call the police and report you. There are laws against con artists like you. Go sell your lies and superstitions somewhere else." She then fixed her gaze back to the floor.

"I'm sorry to have bothered you." I said softly heading back to the other end of the laundry room.

When the washing machine stopped, she placed her wet clothes in the basket and left the laundry. She did not stay to dry them, nor did she look in my direction as she walked past me. It was at that moment I realized her grandmother and infant son had already vanished.

For me, it would be a true statement to say the dead can be very annoying, with their constant intrusions into my life seeking help. I would be visited by her grandmother and son on four more occasions; all occurring in my bedroom. Each time they would just appear at the foot of my bed with the grandmother communicating the same message to me; 'She needs to know her son is loved and cared for.'

Finally, a week later I wrote a short letter and placed it in an envelope and then late one evening I attached it to the Goldman's apartment door since I truly felt uncomfortable in approaching Mark or Linda Goldman in person. It read:

Mr. and Mrs. Goldman,

My name is Evelyn Adams. I know because of your religious beliefs you do not put any faith in what I do as a psychic. Nevertheless, I am going to tell you of a vision I have had from a lady who identifies herself as Margaret, grandmother to Linda Goldman.

She has asked me to convey to both you and your husband the following message from the great beyond. Your son Davin is happy and well and is loved very much. She wants you to know that once a mother gives birth here on earth, from that point up until the approximate age of two years old the new soul that has incarnated into this world through the baby's body has a decision to make. It can choose with its free will to stay and work on the lessons it has chosen for this lifetime or it can back out of that planned life and simply leave and return to the world of spirit.

If it chooses to vacate the body sometime during the first two years of life, for whatever reason, the baby's body simply dies when the soul leaves it. The physical body cannot sustain life without a soul inside and it shuts down. Doctor's who cannot find a medical cause for the death of an infant then call it a Crib Death.

The soul leaves the physical body not to punish the parents, but for its own personal reasons seeking the best life possible to help it advance spiritually.

Margaret wants you two to know the death of your infant son had nothing to do with either of you personally. It was simply its choice to leave for its own personal reasons. So do not blame yourselves for this outcome. There is no fault to be assigned here, none whatsoever.

She and your son love you both very much, but it is time for you both to move on with your lives. God Bless.

It was my great hope the short letter would bring them some comfort in their loss and grief, and maybe bring some understanding to this unfortunate situation.

Their response to my letter came two days later. As I opened the door to very loud knocking, I was stunned to see two Sheriff Deputies standing there. They informed me an official complaint had been made saying I was attempting to use my position as a fortune teller to illicit money fraudulently from the death of the Goldman's son.

They said this was my one and only warning to 'cease and desist' making intrusions into the lives of the Goldman's or face criminal charges. I informed the deputies I would have no further contact of any kind with the Goldman's.

Three days after that incident I received a certified letter from the apartment management stating I had thirty days to vacate my apartment. It listed several reasons for the eviction; namely that I was harassing other tenants with my religious beliefs, that I was operating an unlicensed business from my apartment, that the police had to be summoned to my apartment and that others in the apartment community didn't want me practicing or directing 'black magic' toward them or their children.

After reading the eviction letter I must admit I sat down and cried for nearly an hour. I was so disheartened at how my small gesture had caused such a severe backlash against my open and honest intentions.

Pulling myself together over the next week I began looking for a new residence. Not one to wallow in depression I quickly found my positive footing again and moved on with my life with the assistance of Alexander.

*Note to Readers: Some people say the loss of a child is the most severe loss one can experience, but this is not true. Anyone who loses a mother or father, a wife or husband, a brother or sister, a son or daughter, a true friend or companion, or even a beloved pet; that loss to 'them' may be the most devastating. Each person experiences the loss of a loved one in their own way. No one can measure how much grief we will go through or for how

long it will take us to come to terms with our loss.

Chapter Eight

My friend Madelyn and I crossed paths in the supermarket. We were chit-chatting about her grandkids and the like when she brought up her ailing mother. She would be undergoing testing for liver cancer at the end of the week and as expected she was very afraid indeed. Many still view cancer as a death sentence.

Madelyn asked if they could come for a reading the next day, but I had already made plans to work at a psychic fair in another city and would be staying there for two days. I was leaving early the next morning and told her I would be glad to do it after that, but she had already planned to be with her mother for the testing which was also taking place in another city. They were flying out the day after tomorrow. Therefore, we decided to hook-up the day after their return flight back.

Truly I felt bad not being able to help her mother before seeing her oncology specialist, but I needed the money and many of my regular clients were counting on me being there at the psychic fair.

A week later they were back and after a brief phone call they were on their way to my apartment. They arrived within the hour and after making them comfortable we got down to business.

Madelyn's mother, Bertha was very quiet and seemed to be in the early stages of depression. Just from her demeanor I could tell the cancer testing didn't show any positive results.

Madelyn did most of the talking as her mother seemed very tired and was doing her best at this point to just exist. She confirmed my observations about the test results; that she was basically given a death sentence. Her doctor wants to do a massive round of radiation followed by a heavy dose of chemotherapy but was not very optimistic they would have any effect.

Bertha knew about psychics and the like through her daughter but never put much stock in it. She was raised in the Baptist faith and never truly understood why her daughter left it to seek a new path into Spiritualism. She was not a fan of the so-called 'New Age' reality her daughter was always babbling about, as she put it.

"Well Evelyn, I'm not sure we still need a reading now that the test results are in." Madelyn was patting her mother's knee gently. Her mother just stared off into space with watery eyes.

"Since you're here let me just tune in to my guide and see if he has anything else to offer on this situation. It can't hurt to ask." She started to retrieve some money from her purse, "Oh no dear, put that away. Let's just see if my guide has anything to say."

Madelyn closed her purse and snuggled a bit closer to her mother and held her hand as she spoke, "Okay then."

Alexander started sending me information, "My guide is saying that cancer is a scary word to most humans and that there are many reasons for cancer to appear in someone's life. From a spiritual point of view cancer can make a person take note of a life they are wasting through frivolous life pursuits; cancer in that case pulls them from their complacent lifestyle and refocuses them to what is truly important for their spiritual growth. Cancer allows many to tune in to who they truly are and allows them to forgive themselves as they then seek to live the life they had chosen before being born. Some go on to die because they feel worthless, and some because of self-hate feel they do not deserve to live. Other cancers come into a person's life because of poor diet and lack of exercise; your body is your home so-to-speak and 'you' and only 'you' are responsible for maintaining it. Cancer in and of itself can be a most profound lesson and can be a chosen path for those wishing to use it as a way to leave your world. He says there are many other reasons for cancer, but these will suffice for now. He says most cancers, like many other major diseases are simply here to teach specific life lessons to those who have chosen a certain disease for that very purpose. Don't see cancer or any other disease as a death sentence, but as a learning opportunity. Yes, he says it may lead to death, but that, at times, is what was desired by the soul who is experiencing this disease through the human form; for its spiritual enlightenment."

Madelyn had a look of uncertainty on her sad, tired face as she asked, "So…what type of cancer is my mother experiencing then?"

Alexander answered quickly, "Oh!" I wasn't expecting his response.

"What?" Madelyn chimed in.

"I'm sorry, his answer through me off a bit. He says your mother doesn't have liver cancer; she has been misdiagnosed."

"What?!" Madelyn was also a bit surprised by the answer as I was.

"My guide is saying she needs to go to another doctor for a second opinion. They will confirm the misdiagnosis. He also said if she had undergone the chemotherapy treatment, that the chemo, which is simply a poison, would have caused her organs to start failing. He says she would have succumbed to the treatment, not from any cancer. He says the problem now facing your mother is the shock she is experiencing from the cancer diagnosis. She has lost her will to live. She is so physically, mentally and emotionally drained she has been quietly praying for death to take her to end the misery. Prayers are thoughts and thoughts which are sent out with strong emotion attached to them do bring results; whether positive or negative. She is trying to bring an end to her physical existence through her own free will. This is her right to seek such an ending, and should her spirit companion receive validation from a higher spiritual being; her prayer to die my be allowed to come to fruition depending on whether most of her life lessons have been experienced, and whether she would have the future ability to still accomplish any remaining lessons or not have the ability to do so because of the state she is now in. At this point it could go either way concerning whether she lives on or dies and returns home."

"So, what now?" Madelyn asked with great uncertainty displayed over her weary face.

"My guide says it's all up to her and her spirit companion now. You will know their answer within a few months time he says, one way or the other."

Madelyn helped her mother out as we exchanged 'goodbyes.'

I received a phone call just short of three months later and Madelyn said her mother did confirm the misdiagnosis, but it didn't seem to have any effect on her. Enzyme testing found she just needed to be put on a gluten-free diet. She still did not want to live and nothing her daughter did could pull her out of her deep depression. She had her mother put on anti-depressants, but they seemed to make things worse overall.

As she began to cry, she told me her mother had passed quietly in her sleep just four days ago and asked if I would come to her funeral. I told her I would be there.

* Note to Readers: Do not fear death, for it is simply your Soul returning to your true home. Those you have known throughout eternity; true friends and companions who have been with you through many lifetimes will rejoice when you return to the unseen world. They will be waiting with open arms to receive you and surround you with feelings of pure love and peace at your

return. It matters not what your beliefs are, for we

were all created by the same God.

Chapter Nine

I was happy to hear the news that two friends of mine were becoming engaged and were planning a small marriage. Shortly after hearing this wonderful news I received a phone call from Joni Jones, who simply went by 'JJ.' Young and impetuous, she was the impending bride-to-be and was seeking a reading from me, and I was happy to oblige.

Alan Crane, a very dashing young man was the impending groom and was not coming with her she said because he had to work. So, after her early morning arrival and some girlie chit-chat about the upcoming nuptials we got down to business so-to-speak.

After preparing myself for Alexander's arrival I began, "So JJ what is on your mind?"

"Well, this is a very important step in my life, and I would like to know if Alan is my one and only true soul mate?"

"Alright then, let me see what my guide has to say. First, he wants to give you a better understanding concerning the term soul mate. He says certain souls incarnate for the purpose of interacting specifically with another soul in a specific lifetime. This does not have to be a long-term interaction or a significant interaction; only that the interaction occurs, by both souls agreeing and by positive consideration by those above you. There are some who are soul mates who are engaged in long term relationships and others who only have short involvements with your life. The purpose of these relationships ranges the full spectrum of needs, emotions, and for development, or receiving an experience. He says it is important to know that simply because you are soul mates does not make you 'lovers.' You can have friends and colleagues who are soul mates. Soul mates can refer more to your similarity in progress that has been made through your development as an energy being; your true self. Though, it is possible that there is a link between beings that do not reside in these areas of existence within your true home. He says there

are soul mates who work together on spiritual

progress; often these can be groups, not limited to

just a singular pair of souls. These groups work to

promote and motivate or help to understand the

experiences had by the group for the sake of

evolving and, as you might understand it,

educating each other for the purpose of ascending

to a higher frame of knowledge. Can you follow

what he is saying so far JJ?"

"Yes, I guess so, but does that mean me, and

Alan are true soul mates or not?"

I could tell by her response she wasn't truly

understanding Alexander's message, but more

often then not people hear only what they want to

hear, "Alright JJ, let me see if my guide can clarify it for you. He says it is possible that significant or insignificant relationships also be of your own free will or those that were destined to happen or created to happen for your experience, or even by chance, and that those individuals share nothing in common with you on any plane. Though in many cases, in order for a successful long-term relationship of any kind to take place and be maintained there is often a meaningful accord between the two beyond the physical realm in which you currently reside."

"Evelyn, can your guide simply tell me yes or no, please?"

"Well…he says yes, but…"

"Awesome!" She yelled as she stood up, leaned over and kissed me on the forehead, grabbed her purse and raced out the door. I was stunned for a moment at her response.

Too bad she didn't let me finish what Alexander had to say. He was trying to convey that although Alan is one of her soul mates, he was not here to have a long-term relationship with her. He came into her life to bring her a lesson she requested before they both incarnated. Therefore, their time together would not be long term, not in the way of marriage or as life partners in this lifetime.

Alexander could have told her Alan came into her life to bring a specific lesson; yet he could not tell her what the lesson itself was so as not to influence the outcome of the experience she chose to receive.

I mentally asked Alexander if I should try and convey the rest of his message to her and he said no. Her free will was in play he said so she has the right to move forward with her life, with or without seeking all the information available. Sometimes, actions do speak louder then words.

Chapter Ten

Henry and Loraine Robinson arrived at my apartment knocking softly on my door. They were referred to me by Henry's brother Scott who was a regular client of mine.

They were a pleasant couple in their late thirties and wanted to see if I could shed some light on an incident that happened several months ago concerning their fifteen-year-old son Drew.

Henry had hardly spoken a word while Loraine was doing all the talking. I sensed he wasn't very comfortable, and my impression was his wife made him come with her. I told them I would be glad to see what my guide had to say on the matter.

Loraine told me she was very much into the 'New Age' philosophies and loved reading about psychics, karma, reincarnation and the like. But she said Henry basically thought it was all 'hog wash' as she put it. She laughed as she told me he believed it was all the Devil's work. As she was telling me this Henry made no facial expression; but seemed to be surveying his surroundings as if he truly expected to see a Demon appear from a dark corner.

"So, Loraine, I'm ready to begin if you are?"

"Oh yes, please do."

"So, what was the incident with your son Drew?"

"Well, it was late November and Drew wanted to take Henry's twelve-gauge shotgun and his thirty-eight revolver out by himself and do some target shootin' and maybe a little huntin' to boot.

We live way out in the country where it's mainly woods and corn fields. So, we don't see too many folks out there. So, after Drew pestered his daddy and me for a few days we finally gave in.

He was fifteen and Henry taught him how to handle guns. They had been on many huntin' excursions and whatnot since Drew was twelve. But this was the first time allowin' him to go out by himself, but we felt he was ready. You know how it is; you have to let them fly on their own at some point, so we turned him loose.

It was a cold day, the corn fields had already been ploughed over, so they were muddy and partly frozen in spots, the trees in the wooded areas had no leaves; you get the picture."

"Ah, yes I can visualize what you're saying." I said softly. Henry was now fixated on my face. Just starring with only short eye blinks every now and again; I got the impression he was waiting for me to turn into a witch and fly around the room on a broom. I stayed focused on Loraine and listened as she continued her story.

"Well, Henry and I were in the family room which is on the backside of the house. We have sliding glass doors that look out into the fenced-in back yard. There's a small gate in the far-left corner which leads to the muddy field behind our house. Farther out its all trees and a small creek that snakes through the wooded area.

It was a gray overcast day with the hint of snow in the air. Drew had been out huntin' for about an hour, I guess. We were watchin' TV when Henry saw Drew just standin' outside the little gate. He was just standin' there, in the cold.

Henry brought it to my attention and we both watched Drew just standin' there, not movin'. Then Henry jumped up and started puttin' his boots on and I asked what was goin' on. Henry yelled back as he went out the glass doors that Drew wasn't holdin' the shotgun and that somethin' was wrong. I ran to the doorway and heard Henry callin' Drew's name, but he just stood there like he was in a trance. As Henry opened the gate Drew just seemed to collapse into his arms. Henry carried him back into the house yellin' for me to call 911; Drew's right hand was bloody, and his thumb was missin'.

I told the 911 operator we'd meet the ambulance at the county road, so I wrapped a clean T-shirt around Drew's hand and we loaded up into our pick-up truck. Drew was in shock and basically unconscious. Once the ambulance got him to the hospital, they got everything under

control and said he'd be fine, thank God."

"That must have been a tremendous relief for

you and Henry?" I said. Henry was still watching

me with no expression on his face as Loraine

continued.

"Oh my God, I was so afraid, you just can't

imagine. Henry was just beside himself with

worry." She pulled a tissue from her purse and

dabbed at the tears that had run down her cheeks.

"So, Loraine, what questions do you wish to

ask about?"

"Well, Drew recovered physically pretty much,

but he is a little uncomfortable with his missing

thumb. So, I guess there will always be some

emotional stuff for him to deal with. But Drew has no memory of what happened in the field.

The last thing he remembers is he was bored because there weren't any critters to hunt, so he had been shootin' the revolver at some old soda-pop cans and whatnot until he ran out of bullets. Then he saw a big, half frozen mud puddle and decided to blast it with the shotgun.

He said he remembers firing off a shot which sent mud and water flyin' all over the place. You know how men are; they just love blowin' stuff up. Drew then remembered slidin' the bolt lever back loading another shell into the chamber, but when he aimed at the mud puddle and pulled the trigger, this time he said it didn't go off. Then he said everything just went black. Next thing he

new he woke up in the hospital.

Because his accident involved a gun the

Sheriff's department had a deputy come talk to us

at the hospital, and then sent a deputy to our house

to find the guns since neither were on Drew when

we found him at the back gate.

The sheriff deputy went out our back gate and

traced Drew's foot tracks back to where the guns

were. Both were lyin' on the ground near a single

old tree in the middle of a ploughed-over muddy

corn field. The deputy picked up the guns and

took them to the station as part of their

investigation.

A few weeks later after Drew was back home recuperatin' we got a visit from the deputy who retrieved the guns. He said it would be ruled an accidental shootin' and wanted to know if we wanted the guns back. He said the revolver was fine but that the shotgun was nearly blown in half.

Testing showed he said that the first shot went off okay but when Drew thought he had ejected the spent cartridge, it did not eject and stayed in the chamber. So, when he used the bolt lever to put another shell into the chamber it simply forced the other empty shell to be lodged into the gun barrel. So, when Drew took aim and pulled the trigger the second round had nowhere to go so it exploded, blowing the shotgun almost in half.

The deputy said there were two things their investigation could not account for. First, he said that since Drew was righthanded and had the shotgun up near his head when he pulled the trigger, the resulting explosion should have struck him on the right side of his head, not just his right thumb.

Then he said they also noted when they followed his muddy tracks back to the guns, the tracks ended there. There were no tracks leading back to our house. It looked as if he simply walked out into a muddy field and then vanished. No other footprints could be found anywhere leading back to our house.

Of course, we told him we didn't have any answers either, so he left it at that. We told him we wanted the revolver back, but that they could destroy what was left of the shotgun.

So, we'd like to know if your guide could give us some answers to the deputy's questions."

"Alright, he is saying that many times a person's spirit companion or that which some call their Guardian Angel are connected to the one they watch over through their vibration. If it suddenly changes, they then tune-in so to speak to see what is going on with their charge. Sometimes they are actively observing the person they are charged to oversee.

My guide says he wants you to understand your spirit companion does not spy on those they are watching over, but they are ready if called upon to come forth. For example, it would be like saying your spirit companion is on the second floor of your house and you are in the basement. You can mentally ask for assistance and your spirit companion will get your message. He will receive your request, but he will not be with you in the same room. He will simply send you the answer mentally, as if you were both communicating over the telephone for example. He would not be with you in the same room but would still be connected to you.

Now if you called for help because of a dire situation, then your spirit companion can lower his vibration and leave the second floor of the house to come to you in the basement, so-to-speak if need be. Loraine, are you following what he has said so far?"

"Yes, it makes sense. Go on."

I glanced at Henry, he now had a distant look in his eyes as if he was bored and ready to leave all this 'hog wash.'

Alexander started sending information again, "Alright, my guide says concerning Drew; his spirit companion was aware he was going shooting and was in close contact with him.

218

Drew fired the first time, and then thought he

had ejected the empty cartridge; the empty shell

casing did not eject. It remained in the chamber.

Drew then loaded another shell on top of that

empty one, it was at that moment his spirit

companion then realized what was about to occur.

Drew took aim at the half-frozen mud puddle

and pulled the trigger. Now my guide says you

must understand his spirit companion was in the

spirit world so to speak and your son was in the

physical world.

When the trigger of the shotgun was pulled it

set into motion a physical chain reaction of sorts.

As the gunpowder inside the shell ignited, this

causes the steel pellets to travel at great velocity

down and out the barrel of the gun heading toward its target. But because the barrel was blocked by the empty cartridge the gunpowder which was already in motion had to follow the path of least resistance; that being the weaker outer layer of the gun barrel itself; which is the area that holds the shell in place.

Drew's spirit companion then seeing what was now about to occur materialized a shield of energy and placed that around the ignited shell hoping to contain the blast. The problem was this was a physical event happening in a world of physical matter; Drew's spirit companion did not have enough power so-to-speak to stop the exploding shell, and now realized it could not contain it for very long. At that point he mentally sent out a distress call for Drew's Master Teacher as he is known.

Responding to the distress call, Drew's Master Teacher, who is greatly advanced in spiritual awareness and can call upon greater energy immediately penetrated itself into the physical world and seized the shotgun and forced it down away from Drew's face. As the shell exploded it missed his face but blew his right thumb off.

My guide says had it been possible for the Master Teacher to have arrived sooner, he would have had the power to pull the gun from Drew's hands no matter how tightly he was gripping it, but that the explosion was already in motion and could not be contained at that point in time.

This was just an unforeseen event brought on by humankind's free-will he says. Do you understand Loraine?"

"Yes, it makes sense…so your guide is saying if Drew's Master Teacher had not come, the exploding shell could have blown part of his head off. But what about there being no footprints in the mud leading back to our house. How could he have gotten to the back gate without leaving any trail?"

"My guide says the impact of the shockwave from the blast and the injury to Drew's right hand sent his body into shock. He was virtually rendered unconscious as his body reacted to the sudden incident. His body started to collapse to the ground but was stopped from doing so by his Master Teacher.

This was not a programmed event for Drew to experience in this lifetime, so the intervention was allowed to proceed. To stop the blood loss from his hand and to keep the effects of the shock from killing him his Master Teacher placed a shield of pure oxygen around Drew's body. My guide says he was then pulled up several feet off the ground and levitated to the back gate behind your house.

His Master Teacher then lowered him to a standing position and kept him suspended in that state until your husband then came to his aid.

Once your husband opened the gate the shield was released, and your son collapsed into the arms of his father.

The Master Teacher then withdrew, and the spirit companion then resumed his vigilant watch over his charge. Throughout the three nights Drew spent in the hospital his spirit companion was periodically infusing his body with healing energy. Does that answer your questions Loraine?"

"Oh my god, yes, it does. Thank your guide for his help and thank you Evelyn, you're the best." She leaned over and hugged and then kissed me on the cheek. Henry stood up and his body language made it very clear he was ready to leave my apartment.

They left without saying another word; Loraine was softly crying, and Henry never looked back as they walked out. I was happy Loraine was pleased with the information from Alexander, but I was very relieved when Henry left; that guy creeped-me-out.

*Note to Readers: The Master Teacher is the most advanced energy being that oversees your human experience, and also oversees those who are assigned to assist you during your lifetime. Periodically he observes those who watch over you, and makes any necessary corrections concerning those who assist you. When you reach the point of returning home through the avenue called death, he has the final say as to whether your soul will be allowed to leave your human form, or whether it will remain to complete unfinished lessons. For example, if he determines you have progressed as far as possible, he will then instruct your main spirit companion to shut down the human body and assist your soul in removing itself from it. The death process, depending on the type of death you chose prior to birth can be instantaneous or a long-involved process. Now if you are near death and this was not your chosen time to die, then your Master Teacher will instruct your spirit companion and his helpers to bring forth healing energy to restore your health to a level where you can resume seeking to accomplish more of your chosen lessons. When a situation arises that cannot be handled by your spirit companion then he may call upon your Master Teacher to come forth and solve the problem or dilemma. Keep in mind; all decisions made by your Master Teacher concerning your human existence are for the benefit of your individual 'soul' growth.

Epilogue

These are just some of the experiences I've encountered in my life as a Medium. I hope you have found them as interesting and informative as I have. May God's love and blessings always be in your hearts and minds.

Evelyn Adams

The End

Printed in Great Britain
by Amazon

44412941R00129